Accountability for After-School Care

Devising Standards and Measuring Adherence to Them

Megan Beckett

Angela Hawken

Alison Jacknowitz

Supported by the Stone Soup Child Care Programs

RAND

Labor & Population

The research described in this report was supported by the Stone Soup Child Care Programs.

Library of Congress Cataloging-in-Publication Data

Beckett, Megan.
    Accountability for after-school care : devising standards and measuring
adherence to them / Megan Beckett, Angela Hawken, Alison Jacknowitz.
      p. cm.
    "MR-1411."
    Includes bibliographical references.
    ISBN 0-8330-3072-8
    1. School-age child care—United States—Research. I. Hawken, Angela, 1971–
II. Jacknowitz, Alison, 1972– III. Title.

HQ778.6 .B43 2001
362.7'12'0973—dc21

                         2001048557

RAND is a nonprofit institution that helps improve policy and decisionmaking through research and analysis. RAND® is a registered trademark. RAND's publications do not necessarily reflect the opinions or policies of its research sponsors.

Cover design by Barbara Angell Caslon

Published 2001 by RAND
1700 Main Street, P.O. Box 2138, Santa Monica, CA 90407-2138
1200 South Hayes Street, Arlington, VA 22202-5050
201 North Craig Street, Suite 102, Pittsburgh, PA 15213-1516
RAND URL: http://www.rand.org/
To order RAND documents or to obtain additional information,
contact Distribution Services: Telephone: (310) 451-7002;
Fax: (310) 451-6915; Email: order@rand.org

RAND was asked by Stone Soup Child Care Programs to assess the adherence of its California programs to a set of research-based best practices for after-school care. Toward this end, RAND comprehensively reviewed the literature on after-school programs and derived a set of 18 practices associated with quality of care. We then developed a protocol to measure the extent to which the Stone Soup programs were following these practices, and we applied this protocol to ten randomly selected school campuses with Stone Soup after-school programs.

This report, sponsored by Stone Soup Child Care Programs, RAND's Child Policy Project, and the Promising Practices Network, describes the full project, including the literature review, derivation of practices, and practice-scoring protocols. A companion report, *Measuring Stone Soup's Adherence to After-School Care Practices* (MR-1412.0-SSCCP), summarizes the results of the application as delivered to Stone Soup officials on May 21, 2001.

CONTENTS

FIGURES

TABLES

Several long-term trends have led to increased interest on the part of the American public in how and where children spend their time after school. Among these are the following:

- The percentage of parents at home when school lets out has steadily declined in the past several decades.

- A number of highly publicized violent incidents have occurred involving children and adolescents.

- A move toward academic accountability has increased attention to after-school programs as a means of improving school performance.

In response to these concerns, the number of after-school programs has steadily risen over the past decade. As of the late 1990s, one of every six children aged six to twelve with employed mothers was participating in a before- or after-school program. Increased federal and state funding suggests that the number of such programs will increase in the coming years. In the case of the U.S. Department of Education's 21st Century Community Learning Centers programs, funding increased from $1 million in 1997 to $450 million in 2000, with $1.5 billion proposed for 2002 (Afterschool Alliance, 2001).

Given the proliferation of after-school programs, a greater premium is bound to be placed on information that helps in the design, selection, and management of such programs. With the sponsorship of Stone Soup Child Care Programs and additional support from the RAND Child Policy Project and the Promising Practices Network, we sought to provide information helpful for these purposes in two ways:

- We identified a set of good management practices that currently available evidence and expert judgment indicate should be associated with quality child care.

- As a case study, we assessed the degree to which Stone Soup's programs adhered to these good practices.

IDENTIFYING GOOD PRACTICES

In accomplishing the first task, we assessed the research literature on after-school care in an effort to define good practices. By "good practices," we mean program or process elements that have been shown or upheld by experts in the field to be associated with high-quality after-school programs or with positive child outcomes (e.g., educational attainment, emotional development, and health). Unfortunately, while the stronger empirical work we identified showed an association between practices and desirable outcomes, it failed to establish causal relationships. Most of the publications available for review are not empirical at all but summarize recommendations provided by expert panels and individuals. Thus, judgment has played a strong role in our definition of good practices, and our list must be considered preliminary and subject to change in light of new research.

We initially identified 20 good practices, grouped into three categories as follows:

Staff Management Practices

- Training staff
- Hiring and retaining educated staff
- Providing attractive compensation
- [Keeping turnover rate low]
- [Hiring and retaining experienced staff]

Program Management Practices

- Providing a sufficient variety of activities
- Ensuring that programming is flexible
- Establishing and maintaining a favorable emotional climate
- Maintaining a low child-to-staff ratio
- Keeping total enrollment low
- Having a mix of younger and older children
- Providing age-appropriate activities and materials
- Providing adequate space
- Maintaining a continuity and complementarity with regular day school
- Establishing clear goals and program evaluation
- Providing enough quality materials
- Paying adequate attention to safety and health

Community Contacts

- Involving families
- Using volunteers
- Using community-based organizations and facilities

We eliminated two practice standards (indicated in brackets) because we could find only limited support on their behalf in the literature. We judged three of the standards—the first three program management practices—to have stronger support in the literature than the other standards, because their relationship with positive outcomes was empirically tested in at least one study.

MEASURING ADHERENCE TO PRACTICES: A CASE STUDY

In accomplishing our second task, we developed a measurement methodology and instruments to measure adherence to our list of practice standards and applied them to Stone Soup's child care programs. Stone Soup Child Care Programs is a nonprofit organization that administers school-based after-school programs in collaboration with local school districts, communities, and parents throughout California. The organization is supported by contributions from foundations, corporations and local businesses, government, and individuals.

The stated objective of Stone Soup is to ensure "quality child care for school-age children that is safe, dependable, and affordable through a managed program of shared resources and goals." Stone Soup could satisfy itself through inspection that its programs met almost all these characteristics but believed that a judgment on quality would require external input. Stone Soup recognized that there were not widely accepted quality standards and sought through the current study to help establish some. The organization also sought RAND's independent judgment regarding the extent to which it was meeting the standards and where it might improve.

We concluded that, on average, Stone Soup's programs do a solid job of adhering to good practices. To arrive at this conclusion, we collected administrative data from Stone Soup's central office, surveyed ten randomly chosen site supervisors, and visited those sites to supplement the information collected by survey. On the basis of this information, we rated each program's adherence to each of our good practices according to the paradigm used by the School-Age Care Environment Rating Scale (SACERS), which has been extensively validated and widely used. That paradigm has four grades:

- **Excellent:** high-quality care that expands children's experiences, extends their learning, and provides warm and caring support

- **Good:** developmentally appropriate care

- **Minimal:** custodial-level care

- **Inadequate:** lack of care, i.e., actions compromising children's development

Clearly, this is not a scale on which the typical program will get the highest grade and lesser grades will indicate deficiencies of some sort. "Excellent" care is exceptional and "good" care is still good.

We averaged grades across the ten programs to derive an overall grade for Stone Soup on each practice standard. Stone Soup adhered to the highest standard of care for training staff. The programs were rated minimal on average for hiring and retaining educated staff, providing age-appropriate activities, and using volunteers. It is noteworthy, however, that close adherence to every good practice is not necessarily consistent with other important goals an organization may have. Choices have to be made. Stone Soup tries to hire from the low-income communities it serves, and it provides only part-time hours with modest wages. This choice is likely to constrain staff education to realize value from community participation.

Adherence to the other 14 retained standards was judged good. On 6 of these 14, the 10 program sites we evaluated exhibited substantial variation. Such variation suggested that some sites might not be performing nearly as well as others and that there was thus room for improvement. We offered recommendations for improvement specific to each standard (and also to the standards where adherence was judged minimal).

We recommended to Stone Soup two alternative paths for future re-assessments of adherence to good practices, depending on the objective of the assessment:

- If Stone Soup wants to measure change overall in adherence to the 18 practices (or some subset thereof), it should replicate our study on a random sample of sites. However, this study would need to ensure confidentiality to the site supervisors.

- If Stone Soup wants to identify the sites needing the most improvement on specific practices, it should replicate the full study for all sites. This would obviously be a more expensive approach.

ACKNOWLEDGMENTS

This report benefited greatly from the constructive comments, reviews, and guidance provided by Deborah Vandell (on an earlier version of this report), Jill Cannon, Laura Hamilton, and Rebecca Kilburn. RAND's Child Policy Project and the Promising Practices Network provided support for the preparation of this report. We are grateful to Susan Gates and Tessa Kaganoff for sharing with us their knowledge of the best-practices literature and to Beverly Weidmer for sharing her expertise in questionnaire development. Patrice Lester provided valuable support with preparation of this manuscript. The project as a whole benefited from the individuals who helped with an earlier feasibility study conducted for Stone Soup, including Dan McCaffrey, Lee Mizell, Moira Inkeles, and Alison Jacknowitz. We thank Sally Morton (and the Evidence-Based Center) and Marc Elliott for statistical guidance related to the meta-analysis. James Chiesa made important editorial contributions throughout the preparation of this report (and wrote the accompanying research brief). The school districts, and school principals at each of the sites we visited generously granted us permission to visit the schools, and the site supervisors and assistants at each site we visited kindly shared their insights and experiences. Finally, we are indebted to Stone Soup Child Care Programs' founder/president, Judith G. Brandlin, Stone Soup Executive Director Frank McKendall, and Stone Soup board members Shizuko Akasaki, Scott Bice, Esq., Norma L. Gonzales, Lynda W. Griffith, Ph.D., Russell O'Neill, Ph.D., and June Sale for their ongoing assistance and guidance throughout the project.

ASES   After-School Environmental Scale

ASQ   Assessment of School-Age Child Care Quality

ERIC   Educational Resources Information Centers

GED   General Equivalency Diploma

JSTOR   Journal Storage: The Scholarly Journal Archive

NAEYC   National Association for the Education of Young Children

NICHD   National Institute of Child Health and Human Development

SACERS   School-Age Care Environment Scale

SES   Socioeconomic status

Chapter One

INTRODUCTION

Several long-term trends have led to increased interest on the part of the American public in how and where children spend their time after school. First, the percentage of parents at home when school lets out has steadily declined over the past several decades. A second trend is the growing number of highly publicized violent incidents involving children and adolescents. Third, a move toward academic accountability has increased attention to after-school programs as a means of improving school performance.

In response to these concerns, the number of after-school programs has steadily risen over the past decade. In 1997, 16 percent of children aged six to twelve years with employed mothers participated in a before- or after-school program (Capizzano, Tout, and Adams, 2000). Increased federal and state funding suggests that the number of such programs will increase in the coming years. For example, funding for the U.S. Department of Education's 21st Century Community Learning Centers programs increased from $1 million in 1997 to $40 million in 1998 and $450 million in 2000 (National Research Council and Institute of Medicine, 2000).

Given the growing interest in and funding for after-school programs, it has become important to be able to identify which programs are effectively designed and managed. Sponsors need reassurance that they are supporting programs that are benefiting the children, parents, and communities they are serving.

RAND was commissioned by Stone Soup Child Care Programs, a nonprofit organization that administers school-based after-school programs throughout California, to measure the adherence of its after-school programs to a set of recognized practices. Three tasks were carried out to achieve this objective. Task 1 was a thorough review of the published after-school care literature to identify practices that are generally accepted as characteristic of quality care. Task 2 involved the design and implementation of a data collection effort to measure adherence of a sample of the sponsor's after-school programs to the practices identified in Task 1. Task 3 involved analyzing the data collected as part of Task 2 and summarizing the results.

We anticipate that this report, which summarizes the final product of the three tasks, will prove useful to researchers, practitioners, and funding organizations with an interest in after-school care. Chapter One provides a systematic assessment of the state-of-the-art knowledge of after-school care and recognized practices. For practitioners, this will provide a guide to the processes and outcomes that are widely considered to be indicative of quality care. For researchers and funding organizations, it may serve as a useful and systematic summary of the state of the current knowledge base while also highlighting the lack of solid empirical research as to what characteristics of programs are associated with positive student outcomes. Chapters Two and Three summarize the approach we took to measuring adherence to the practices identified in Task 1 and the types of analyses that can shed light on a program's strengths and weaknesses. These chapters will be useful for practitioners or funding organizations interested in evaluating how well after-school care programs are adhering to currently recognized practices.

Chapter Two

IDENTIFYING AFTER-SCHOOL CARE PRACTICES

APPROACHES TO IDENTIFYING PRACTICES

In designing our approach to identifying practices, we turned first to the business literature in which methods for deriving the concept originated. "Best practices," in business terminology, refer to documented strategies and tactics used by better-performing companies.[1] A small industry consisting of organizations and consultants has emerged to help business executives identify and implement practices that can improve their own organizations.[2] The approaches taken vary across practitioners but generally consist of identifying a list of organizations that are top performers in their class and approaching these top performers about participating in the study. Site visits are then made to organizations that agree to participate, and data on factors or enablers that are perceived as contributing to an organization's success are collected and analyzed. These results are summarized across participating organizations, and a list of best practices is distilled. Experts in the area or industry are integral to each step of this process, from the identification of top-performing organizations to the collection and analysis of best practices.

In the public policy arena as it applies to educational programs, government agencies and other groups rely on expert panels consisting of subject matter experts. Depending on the issue at hand, expert panels may be charged with identifying "exemplary programs" or

---

[1]See, for example, http://www.best-in-class.com/site_tools/faq.htm#best_practice.

[2]An example is the American Productivity & Quality Center.

3

"effective innovations" and must therefore be familiar with the programs being assessed. Sometimes, less formal workshops consisting of subject matter experts are convened to review the current knowledge base in a particular area. A recent example was a workshop convened by the Board on Children, Youth, and Families to review the state of the knowledge base on after-school programs for children and adolescents aged five to fourteen and the implications for the next generation of after-school programs (National Research Council and Institute of Medicine, 2000). Experts participating in these panels and workshops are a mix of academics and practitioners in the field.

For this project, we adapted a different approach to identifying practices:[3] meta-analysis.[4] Meta-analysis is the systematic collection, assessment, and presentation of all relevant and quality evidence on a particular subject. A meta-analysis is a "specific methodologic and statistical technique for combining quantitative data" that produces a statistical inferential statement such as a confidence interval or a statistical test (Mulrow, Cook, and Davidoff, 1998). As such, a meta-analysis is a final step one may take in a systematic review if appropriate. Technically we are not using meta-analysis in this process because the evidence (or publications) we identified in this small substantive field has too few quality studies that meet the standards for being included in a traditional meta-analysis. Thus, we are not able to draw formal inferences to a larger population. Instead, we quantitatively synthesize all the relevant literature in a way that is based on traditional meta-analysis. We will use the term *meta-analysis* for our quantitative synthesis throughout this document.

---

[3]We use the term *practices* rather than *best practices* because, as will be seen, the quality and quantity of evidence vary substantially with respect to different practices and because one of the chief tasks we are undertaking is to assess the evidence behind a particular practice—not all practices meet the criteria of "best practice." Indeed, given the paucity of solid empirical studies examining particular practices in the literature today, we are uncomfortable applying the term best practice to any of the practices considered in the meta-analysis and thus apply a different set of labels, as explained later in this chapter.

[4]To our knowledge, we are the first to construct the meta-analysis algorithm used in this publication. As we state in the text, all the examples of meta-analysis we have encountered are restricted to literatures that contain a moderate body of empirical work of greater statistical rigor than currently exists in the after-school care literature.

Because our method relies solely on publications rather than on subject matter experts, it is less prone to real or perceived subjectivity on the part of the individuals making recommendations.[5] The reasons for this selection were twofold. First, in our initial reading of the literature, we observed that a large percentage of the literature was based on proceedings from workshops or expert panels brought together to identify practices or characteristics of quality programs. What was missing was a systematic assessment and integration of these reports with the small empirical literature, which meta-analysis permits. Second, our scan of the literature indicated that the limited number of studies that evaluate the effectiveness of after-school program characteristics precludes a confident identification of what works and what does not. Rather, the best we can do is identify program features for which there is strong, moderate, or limited support of their effectiveness. This evidence is a combination of expert panel reports and empirical research. By adapting the meta-analysis approach, we were able to derive weights reflecting the consistency of evidence in support of a particular practice.

OUR META-ANALYTIC APPROACH

Meta-analysis involves four principal steps (Shekelle and Morton, 2000):

1. Identification of studies/reports

2. Assessment of studies/reports for quality

3. Organizing studies/reports into sensible groups

4. Summarizing the results

Our first task was to locate the relevant major studies and reports. We scanned the major library databases and indices, including the Educational Resources Information Center (ERIC), JSTOR, and the Social Science Index, for published articles and books. We also reviewed the references in major articles pertaining to after-school

---

[5]However, the published manuscripts that are being evaluated may not always be free of charges of subjectivity, particularly when these manuscripts are themselves based on expert opinions rather than on empirical research.

care. In addition, we searched the database of RAND publications and resources (including the Promising Practices Network) as well as those of government agencies (e.g., the National Research Council, the National Institute of Child Health and Development, and the U.S. Departments of Education and Justice), professional associations of educators and child care workers (e.g., the National Association of Elementary School Principals, the National Child Care Association, and the National Association for the Education of Young Children [NAEYC]), and other relevant nonprofit foundations, organizations, and associations (e.g., the Carnegie Corporation of New York, the David and Lucile Packard Foundation, the National Institute on Out-of-School Time, the National Network for Child Care, and Fight Crime: Invest in Kids). Results from this literature search produced a combination of empirical research studies (studies attempting to link characteristics of after-school programs or staff with child/parent/ program outcomes) and reports produced by professional organizations or by expert panels.

Next, we scanned the resources gathered in the first stage to identify further potentially relevant reports or research articles. In a number of reports we scanned, the authors cited sources to back their recommendations for practices. When possible, we tried to obtain these cited articles so as to be able to assess a practice based on the original sources. Our approach is conservative in that we restricted the studies and reports in our review to published manuscripts that in the case of the research studies have undergone peer review. Unlike traditional meta-analysis, which includes only those studies that meet a minimum quality threshold, we included in our literature assessment all publications that relate to after-school care practices.

The second step was to read and assess the quality of each paper or report to determine its weight in the meta-analysis. To do so, we derived a classification rule that assigns papers and reports to one of four categories.[6] The category of publications in which we have the

---

[6]This hierarchy is a modification of the standard "hierarchy of evidence" (Canadian Task Force on the Periodic Health Examination, 1979) used in meta-analysis. The standard hierarchy is as follows: (1) randomized controlled trial; (2) well-designed cohort or case-control study; (3) comparison between times or places with and without intervention; and (4) expert opinion. Modifications usually put case studies and panels in category IV.

greatest confidence are *Tier 1 publications.* Tier 1 publications are generally journal articles that present original empirical research attempting to establish relationships between one or more program features and one or more child/parent/program outcomes. If a statistically significant and positive association is found, the program features are for our purposes considered a practice. Tier 1 publications use a formal study design and employ a control of some type to adjust for the unobserved processes by which children were selected into a program.

Tier 2 publications refer to reports produced by formal expert panels or by workshops convened to identify exemplary after-school programs or practices as well as reports produced by professional organizations. Recommendations produced in these reports are distinguished by the use of multiple subject matter experts (in contrast to a single expert), who presumably bring a greater breadth and depth of knowledge to the task of making recommendations than can a single expert or author. We included two literature reviews in this category because implicit in any review is the compilation of expertise and findings based on multiple experts or authors who wrote the papers and reports being reviewed.[7] A major limitation of publications in Tier 2 is that it is impossible to assess whether a recommendation is based on experience and knowledge or if it represents advocacy, as is the case for calls to increase staff salaries in the broader education literature.[8]

Tier 3 publications are empirical studies in that they involve original data collection (which may consist of an in-depth interview with a child participant or with program staff). On the basis of these data, the researcher attempts to draw some type of conclusion about the association between a practice and program or child outcomes, but the statistical rigor of this analysis is substantially weaker than

---

[7]In the literature reviews and in some of the expert panel reports, there are explicit references to some of the Tier 1 and Tier 3 publications we reviewed, thus causing us to overweight such publications. In other expert panel reports, the text suggests that some of the publications we consider are being referred to, but attribution is not made. Because we opted to be overly inclusive, we took the naïve approach of treating recommendations made in all literature reviews and expert panel reports equally.

[8]We thank Laura Hamilton for drawing our attention to this parallel in the more general education literature.

that for Tier 1 articles. For example, there may not be sufficient variation across programs in a practice to permit statistical testing for a practice-outcome association. In essence, these "studies" draw conclusions about which practices are associated with better care without presenting supporting statistics. We assume this "evidence" is based on the experience of the author and assign less weight than is assigned to Tier 2 publications, which are based on the experience and knowledge of the literature of an expert panel.

Tier 4 publications present the assumptions or experiences of a single expert or practitioner (versus the perspectives of multiple experts or authors). These publications are assigned the least weight because of the ambiguity surrounding whether the recommendation is based on experience or is an assumption of the writer.

The breakdown by tier of the publications included in the meta-analysis is provided in Table 2.1. We also reviewed other papers that are not included in the meta-analysis because they (1) were based on early child care, or (2) evaluated the benefits of participating in after-school care vis-à-vis other forms of care. The meta-analysis includes only studies or reports that consider specific practices or characteristics of after-school care programs.

In traditional meta-analysis, one summarizes the magnitude of an effect of an intervention or practice. This is undesirable in our case, as both the quantity and the quality of the after-school care empirical research are markedly less than that normally analyzed using meta-analysis, restricting us to only a few studies (i.e., the two Tier 1 publications).[9] For example, a typical meta-analysis in the social sciences initially examined over 300 articles addressing the question of whether patient education in chronic illness helped therapeutically

---

[9]Although we attempted to replicate the meta-analysis based on those papers which reported "failure to find" effects as well as significant program features' effects on student and parent outcomes, we were stymied by the very small number of studies and the inconsistent predictor variables used in these few papers. When we did a meta-analysis, none of the program features emerged as a practice. We considered incorporating information on failure to find results in our meta-analysis, but because by definition none of the Tier 2–4 publications discuss practices that are not considered important, incorporating these results would have resulted in a double standard of what information is allowed in each tier. A more traditional meta-analytic approach on after-school care practices will have to await more empirical research on the topic.

Table 2.1

Papers by Category Included in the Meta-Analysis

	Category			
	Tier 1	Tier 2	Tier 3	Tier 4
Number of papers	2	14	8	1

(Mazzuca, 1982, cited in Wolf, 1986). The first step in this meta-analysis involved subsetting down to the 30 empirical studies that used a true experimental design (i.e., those designs that randomly assigned subjects to a treatment or control group). In contrast, our review of the literature identified a total of 25 articles or reports on after-school care practices, 10 of which are empirical and none of which employed a true experimental design. Of the empirical studies, two met the Tier 1 criteria. Given the limitations of the literature on after-school care, rather than summarize the magnitude of the effects of a practice, we loosened the criteria of reports to be assessed to include all reports addressing specific characteristics of after-school care programs.

For our third step, we organized studies according to the practice being evaluated or recommended. This resulted in 20 specific practices that we further classified into three broad categories: staff characteristics, program characteristics, and community contacts. A practice had to be referred to in at least three publications to make it into our list of potential practices.

Our last step consisted of empirically summarizing the results of the meta-analysis. Our approach involved several stages. First, for each study we assigned binary indicators of whether an effect of a practice is found or a practice is recommended. A critical component of how we identified this measure was that the absence of a mention of a particular practice constituted a failure to "find" an effect. This is sensible with Tier 2 publications, which include literature reviews. It may not be as reasonable for Tier 1 and Tier 3 studies because they may not address a particular topic. On the positive side, the strict criterion that we are applying to Tier 1 and Tier 3 studies will downwardly bias the level of support to counteract the level of support provided by the well-recognized phenomenon of publication bias.

Publication bias refers to the fact that there is a strong tendency for academic journals to publish empirical research that finds an effect but not to publish research that fails to do so. In other words, the Tier 1 and Tier 3 studies we identified in all likelihood underrepresent empirical work that fails to find a relationship between a practice and an outcome.

Second, we assigned weights in order to combine this information. The weights reflect the relative importance we assigned to an effect based on the tier of the publication. Traditionally, meta-analysis assigns greater weight to studies with less variance, which generally means that studies with larger sample sizes receive greater weight or, alternatively, that more accurate studies receive more weight. Meta-analysts also commonly use study quality scores to stratify on, excluding, for example, lower-quality studies, or conducting sensitivity analyses to determine whether quality affects the conclusions. Sample size is available only for Tier 1 and Tier 3 studies, not for Tier 2 and Tier 4 reports. Thus, we assigned weights to the different tiers that reflected our intuition about their relative accuracy. We started with a weighting scheme that assigned the greatest weight (0.45) to Tier 1 publications, the next-greatest weight to Tier 2 (0.35) followed by Tier 3 studies (0.15), and the least weight to the single-authored Tier 4 recommendations (0.05). The sum of the weights equals 1.0.

For each practice, we multiplied the percentage of publications within a tier by the weight. For example, 50 percent (1 of 2) of Tier 1 publications, 21 percent (3 of 14) of Tier 2, 13 percent (1 of 8) of Tier 3, and 0 percent (0 of 1) of Tier 4 publications support higher education level as a practice, yielding a combined score of $(0.50 \times 0.45) + (0.21 \times 0.35) + (0.13 \times 0.15) + (0 \times 0.05) = 0.32$. We obtained crude scores for each practice by this method. The unstandardized mean score derived from this method was 0.28 with a standard deviation of 0.20. Those practices that stood out from other practices having substantially stronger or substantially weaker support were identified by the standard statistical convention of standard deviations. Thus, practices with a score one standard deviation below the mean were classified as having limited support in the literature; practices with a score within one standard deviation of the mean were considered as having moderate support; and practices with a score at least one standard deviation above the mean were considered as having strong support.

Next, we looked at the contribution to the scores by tier to assess whether one tier exerted undue influence on the final rankings. We determined that this was the case with Tier 2 publications. This is because each Tier 2 report (which presents recommendations produced by expert panels or summarizes literature reviews) on average supports more practices than any other type of publication.[10] In other words, our criterion of binary yes/no support is not necessarily equivalent across criteria.[11] In order to adjust scoring so that each criterion contributed equally to the final weight, we restandardized the scores.[12] The final scores and resulting classification of practices by whether they had strong, moderate, or limited support were consistent with the unstandardized ranks indicating that our approach is robust. The final score column in Table 2.2 shows the standardized final scores. The standardized mean score is 0.28 (0.22 standard deviation).

We performed a final sensitivity check to test the robustness of our results to alternative sets of weights. In particular, we were interested in examining how sensitive our final recommended practices were to assigning greater weight to Tier 1 publications and to narrowing the gap between the tiers. Our results are generally robust. Under the most extreme scenario we examined (Tier 1 weight = 0.60; Tier 2 weight = 0.30; Tier 3 weight = 0.07; and Tier 4 weight = 0.03), the list of strongly supported, moderately supported, and weakly supported practices are the same as those presented in Table 2.2; only when Tier 1 weights are 0.70 or higher do changes result. In particular, more practices drop from moderately supported to weakly supported. Under no scenario we tried did the list of strongly supported practices change. What this means is that our results are not highly dependent on the relative weights we assign to each tier until the weights are extremely tilted in favor of the two Tier 1 studies.

---

[10]This is not surprising given that the purpose of the expert panels and literature reviews, in contrast to association studies, is to scan a large array of practices.

[11]The average percentage of Tier 2 publications consistent with a practice across all practices was 0.47, compared with an average level of support of 0.20, 0.21, and 0.20 for Tiers 1, 3, and 4, respectively.

[12]We divided the initial scores by the average level of support provided by a class of publications across all practices.

Table 2.2

Results of the Meta-Analysis

Practice	Tier[a] 1	2	3	4	Final Score[b]	Final Ranking[c]
Staff characteristics						
Training staff	0	11	2	1	0.23	Moderate
Education	1	3	1	0	0.40	Moderate
Compensation	0	5	0	0	0.09	Moderate
Turnover rate	0	1	1	0	0.05	Limited
Experience	0	3	0	0	0.06	Limited
Program characteristics						
Variety of activities	1	10	5	1	0.61	Strong
Flexibility of programming	1	8	2	1	0.50	Strong
Emotional climate	2	11	4	0	0.92	Strong
Child-to-staff ratio	1	7	2	0	0.49	Moderate
Total enrollment	1	4	1	0	0.42	Moderate
Mixing of age groups	1	2	1	1	0.39	Moderate
Age-appropriate activities	0	6	1	0	0.13	Moderate
Space availability	0	7	2	0	0.17	Moderate
Continuity and complementarity with day school programs	0	8	4	0	0.28	Moderate
Clear goals and evaluation of program	0	9	1	0	0.17	Moderate
Materials	0	6	2	0	0.16	Moderate
Attention to safety and health	0	9	2	0	0.20	Moderate
Community contacts						
Involvement of families	0	10	1	0	0.19	Moderate
Use of volunteers	0	4	1	0	0.10	Moderate
Partnerships with community-based organizations, etc.	0	8	0	0	0.13	Moderate
Total number of studies	2	14	8	1		
Standardized mean score	0.28	0.28	0.30	0.28	0.28	
Standard deviation					0.22	

[a]Numbers signify the total number of studies in a given category supporting a practice (e.g., 0 of 2 Tier 1 publications support training staff as a practice).

[b]See the text for a discussion of how this score is calculated.

[c]Strong support is assigned to final scores that are at least one standard deviation above the grand mean; moderate support is defined as a final score within one standard deviation of the grand mean; and limited support is defined as a final score that falls below one standard deviation of the grand mean.

Research on after-school care practices is lagging behind the growing interest in and public resources devoted to after-school care programs. This means that most of what are commonly accepted as good management practices in after-school care literature are based on assumptions and experiences of practitioners rather than solid research. The modified meta-analytic approach presented in this chapter allows for a systematic quantitative synthesis of a social services literature in which only 2 of 25 relevant publications met the threshold for inclusion in a standard meta-analysis.

THE PRACTICES

The after-school care practices examined are divided into three primary categories: staff characteristics, program characteristics, and community contacts. Examples of staff characteristics include staff experience, education, and training staff. Program characteristics refer to those elements that reflect the program's environment, including total enrollment, space, and adequacy of materials. Community contacts refer to interactions between the program and the community, such as the use of volunteers. The practices examined in our meta-analysis are those most often referred to in the after-school care literature and therefore those about which the most is known or assumed by experts in the field. In addition, we discuss a fourth category, labeled "other," that includes practices that have been identified as possibly important but about which much less is known. These present possible future practices that may emerge when the field of knowledge about after-school care programs is further developed.

Each summary below assesses the level of confidence in each practice as indicated by the results of the meta-analysis; describes what, if anything, is known about the current status of a practice across programs; and discusses what the literature has to say based on empirical evidence or the experience of experts in the field.

Staff Management Characteristics

Training Staff. Training staff refers to providing staff with additional skills to improve outcomes for program participants. This may include "in-house" training, where the expertise of staff members is shared among colleagues, or external training, which could include classes at community colleges and training partnerships with the affiliated school or other after-school care centers (Walter, Caplan, and McElvain, 2000). The training regimen may include both formal classroom instruction and instruction in areas such as child development and learning, teaching methods, conflict resolution, multicultural awareness, child observation, assessment, and adapting to the needs of children of different ages and those with disabilities (Halpern, 1991; Walter, Caplan, and McElvain, 2000; U.S. Departments of Education and Justice, 2000). Training staff is thought to be associated with several positive results: It may increase the staff's ability to develop and implement developmentally appropriate curriculum; may provide staff with the skills to support and encourage curiosity and exploration (without dominating or interfering), to foster a healthy self-image, and to support the function of staff as role models (Alexander, 1986); and may attract and retain high-quality staff (Fashola, 1998; National Research Council and Institute of Medicine, 2000; U.S. Departments of Education and Justice, 2000). Most after-school programs (about 90 percent) had provided some of their paid staff training in the past year (RMC Corporation, 1993).

Eleven Tier 2 studies, two Tier 3 reports, and one Tier 4 publication recommend training staff as a practice, yielding a moderate level of support for this practice. Although the literature shows a moderate level of support for training staff, the particulars about staff training recommended vary considerably, ranging from very general to specific. Some studies recognize that the type of training required depends on the characteristics and circumstances of the program. Consideration thus needs to be given to what training is required by an organizational authority, such as the school district or licensing agency, staff training requests, skill set requirements given program goals, and what internal and external training options are available (Walter, Caplan, and McElvain, 2000). At a minimum, it is recommended that programs provide orientation and ongoing training for new staff and volunteers (National Institute on Out-of-School Time, 2000; National Association of Elementary School Principals, 1999; National School-Age Care Alliance, 1998). As part of a formal training program, at least one Tier 3 study concludes that implementation of a mentoring system that matches experienced workers with new staff is an important aspect of training (Halpern, 1991).

Staff Education. Much of the research reviewed refers to the benefits of having a "well-prepared" staff; education plays a large role in preparation. Formal education is thought to increase caregivers' breadth of knowledge, cognitive sophistication, internalization of child-oriented values and beliefs, and professionalism (Austin, 1981; Berk and Berson, 1981). In a recent national survey of before- and after-school programs, over half of program directors (62 percent) and about one-third of other senior staff with the most years of formal education had at least a bachelor's degree (RMC Corporation, 1993).

The meta-analysis yields a moderate level of support for the employment of more educated staff as a practice (one Tier 1 publication, three Tier 2 studies, and one Tier 3 publication). In the one Tier 1 study that examines the relationship between program features and observations of children's experiences and perceptions of the program, researchers observed significantly more frequent negative interactions between staff and children in programs with less educated staff (Rosenthal and Vandell, 1996). In this study, staff education varied from a high school diploma to a bachelor's degree. Tier 2 publications suggest that a qualified staff is an essential element of a successful after-school program (U.S. Departments of Education and Justice, 2000; National School-Age Care Alliance, 1998) and, in particular, that staff should meet requirements that are both specific to school-age child care and relevant to their particular jobs (National School-Age Care Alliance, 1998). In this report, "qualified" is a term that encompasses staff education, training, and compensation.

Staff Compensation. Low compensation is widely considered to be a factor in high turnover rates (RMC Corporation, 1993) as well as a negative influence on the morale and motivation of staff. The meta-analysis yields moderate evidence in support of staff compensation as a practice, although it should be noted that with a score of 0.09, this practice just barely made the "moderate" threshold. We suspect that the reason compensation was mentioned in only four Tier 2 reports (Walter, Caplan, and McElvain, 2000; National Research Council and Institute of Medicine, 2000; National School-Age Care Alliance, 1998; U.S. Departments of Education and Justice, 2000) and in none of the empirical studies is that the broader education litera-ture has not linked compensation with any quality outcomes (including retention or turnover). In some cases, calls for greater staff compensation may be a form of advocacy. In light of this fact, we recommend that the inclusion of compensation as a practice be done cautiously.

Staff Turnover Rate. The meta-analysis indicates limited support for low staff turnover as a practice. This practice is often referred to as a beneficial outcome of alternative practices, such as increased com-pensation or training staff, rather than as a policy lever in itself. Re-sults based on a Tier 3 study suggest that staff turnover rates can in-fluence the eventual decision by child and parent to remove a child from the after-school program (Belle, 1997). Staff turnover rates in after-school care centers are high (RMC Corporation, 1993) and can result in understaffing. Program directors participating in the *National Study of Before- and After-School Programs* (RMC Corporation, 1993) report that it took 23 days on average to replace staff members who had resigned. Several factors are believed to contribute to high staff turnover, including low compensation, long hours of service, few career development opportunities, and a limited sense of pro-fessionalism owing to the relative newness of the school-age child care career field (National Association of Elementary School Princi-pals, 1999).

There are several reasons staff turnover rates did not emerge as a strong or moderately supported practice for after-school care. First, neither of the Tier 1 studies examined staff turnover as a predictor. Second, many of the Tier 2 publications we reviewed treat staff turnover as an outcome that may be influenced (i.e., reduced) by other factors, such as staff training and compensation. We concur that staff turnover is more likely to be thought of as an undesirable organizational outcome that raises the recruiting and training staff costs of a program and may be detrimental to children's experiences. Nonetheless, staff turnover is only indirectly under the control of a program (operating through other practices that are not yet well ex-plicated).

Staff Experience. The meta-analysis provides limited support for hiring experienced staff as a practice. Experienced staff are those who have worked with school-age or younger children in a paid or unpaid capacity and who presumably bring at least some of the skills or knowledge of child development that training is believed to confer. The National School-Age Care Alliance defines "related experience" as work with school-age children in recreation, fine arts, camping, or academic settings. None of the empirical studies addressed the benefits associated with hiring experienced staff. Nonetheless, three Tier 2 studies advocate hiring and maintaining experienced staff; in particular, the National School-Age Care Alliance (1998) recommends that all staff be professionally qualified to work with children and youth, including experience with school-age children in recreational settings.

Program Management Characteristics

Variety of Activities. Providing a variety of activities that are age-appropriate and interesting is a strongly supported practice that is cited in one Tier 1, ten Tier 2, five Tier 3, and one Tier 4 publication. The most frequently offered activities (on a daily basis) in a national survey of before- and after-school programs were socializing (97 percent of programs), free time (95 percent), games (89 percent), reading (86 percent), time for homework (81 percent), physically active play (81 percent), and arts and crafts (61 percent) (RMC Corporation, 1993). Some authors believe that offering an array of activities yields several benefits, including the fostering of decisionmaking skills and creativity (Alexander, 1986); time and space for physical play such as running, jumping, and climbing as well as time for the emotional release that art, dramatic play, and sand and water play provide (Alexander, 1986); and the capturing of participants' interests and subsequent increased retention rates (Belle, 1997), particularly at older ages.

There is some empirical support for the asserted benefits derived from a variety of activities. In one Tier 1 study, Rosenthal and Van-dell (1996) conclude that in programs where directors reported a larger number of different activities offered in a week, researchers more frequently observed positive or neutral staff-child interactions,[13] and children's perceptions of the overall climate of the pro-

---

[13]In this study, staff-child interactions are treated as an outcome. It should be noted that this outcome is also a practice.

gram and emotional support received from staff were higher. In the *National Study of Before-and After-School Programs* (RMC Corporation, 1993), the authors found that the choices available for recreational and leisure time appear to be more limited among programs that received the poorest overall quality ratings. Programs that received the highest-quality ratings were more likely to provide creative arts and crafts, science activities, dramatic play, storytelling, role playing, and music on a daily basis. They were also more likely to provide cooking and food preparation by children on a weekly basis (RMC Corporation, 1993). The reader should keep in mind, however, that the quality ratings calculated in this study are based on the factors that were related to quality, including the number of activities provided. In other words, on average, higher-quality programs by definition provide a greater variety of activities than do programs rated lower quality in this study.[14] Finally, one of the Tier 3 studies is consistent with the assumption that the number of available activities is a crucial factor in the child's decision to exit the after-school care system (Belle, 1997).

Flexibility of Programming. Flexibility of programming, referring to the freedom of children to choose among an array of interesting activities (or to select being alone if desired), is strongly supported as a practice. Alexander (1986) argues that programs should ensure that they are not extensions of the tightly scheduled workday and that children do not spend the majority of their out-of-school time in highly structured environments. Another report recommends that at least some of the after-school programming provide time for children to be on their own, away from adult direction as long as clear rules and supervision are provided (Miller and Marx, 1990). Fashola (1998) cautions, however, that if after-school programs aim to enhance academic achievement, structure is essential. Fashola's review of successful academic programs illustrates that these programs had clear goals as well as structured materials and training procedures.

One Tier 1 study, eight Tier 2 reports, two Tier 3 publications, and one Tier 4 study support this practice. In the first of the Tier 1 studies, Pierce, Hamm, and Vandell (1999) found that greater

---

[14]This definitional problem is why the *National Study of Before- and After-School Programs* is classified among the Tier 3 studies.

program flexibility is associated with improved social skills among boys (but not girls). In the *National Study of Before- and After-School Programs* (RMC Corporation, 1993), programs that were assessed as lower-quality tended to be more rigid and less likely to provide children the choice to follow their own interests or curiosity, explore other cultures, or develop hobbies. Children in these lower-quality programs were not encouraged to try new activities, think for themselves, ask questions, or test new ideas.

Emotional Climate (Staff Positivity/Negativity). The meta-analysis strongly supports a positive emotional climate as a practice; this includes fostering a warm relationship between staff and students and between staff and parents as well as positive staff-staff relations (RMC Corporation, 1993; National School-Age Care Alliance, 1998). A positive emotional climate also entails encouraging and respecting students; making children feel welcome, relaxed, and safe (National Research Council and Institute of Medicine, 2000; National Association of Elementary School Principals, 1999; National School-Age Care Alliance, 1998); and fostering mutual respect among staff and volunteers (National Institute on Out-of-School Time, 2000). A positive emotional climate may be especially important for those children without support, guidance, or stable relationships with adults at home (U.S. Departments of Education and Justice, 2000). Finally, several reports advise that a program can establish a positive emotional climate by hiring staff that are warm and caring toward students and that take the time to establish a relationship (Miller and Marx, 1990; National School-Age Care Alliance, 1998; Newman et al., 2000) or by providing training (National Association of Elementary School Principals, 1999).

Eleven Tier 2 publications emphasize the importance of emotional climate, and two Tier 1 and four Tier 3 publications lend some empirical support to the advantages of a positive emotional climate. In one Tier 1 study, the number of negative staff-child interactions observed in programs was positively correlated with children's perceptions of overall climate and emotional support.[15] Further, researcher-observed positive or neutral staff-child interactions were

---

[15]This study is an example of the use of emotional support (as reported from different perspectives) as both a practice and an outcome within the same study.

positively correlated with the autonomy/privacy that children experienced in a program (Rosenthal and Vandell, 1996). In the second Tier 1 study, staff "positivity" (i.e., the extent to which staff appeared to enjoy the children) reduced the internalizing and externalizing of problems for boys, while staff negativity was associated with poor grades in reading and math for boys (Pierce, Hamm, and Vandell, 1999). No significant effects were found for girls. In a separate Tier 3 study, programs that were assessed by outside observers to be of higher quality also scored consistently high in the area of staff-child relations (RMC Corporation, 1993). The authors of this study observed that staff-child interactions set the tone of the program by providing children with role models as well as techniques for making decisions, resolving conflicts, solving problems, accepting their own and others' feelings, and developing a sense of control over their own environment.

Child-to-Staff Ratio. A low child-to-staff ratio may increase the likelihood that children have one-on-one time with an adult and develop a personal relationship with an adult in the center. According to the *National Study of Before- and After-School Programs* (RMC Corporation, 1993), the national average child-to-staff ratio is 8.9:1. Private for-profit programs have the lowest average ratio (6.9:1), whereas public and private nonprofit programs have higher average ratios of 11.4:1 and 9.0:1, respectively.

One Tier 1, seven Tier 2, and two Tier 3 publications emphasize the importance of child-to-staff ratio, yielding a moderate level of support for this practice. A 15:1 ratio for children over six years of age emerges as the most commonly recommended maximum ratio (National Association of Elementary School Principals, 1999; National Institute on Out-of-School Time, 2000; U.S. Departments of Education and Justice, 2000; National School-Age Care Alliance, 1998).

Rosenthal and Vandell (1996) reported that classes with more staff per child had less observed negative staff-child interaction and better parental ratings of the quality of the programs. The *National Study of Before- and After-School Programs* (RMC Corporation, 1993) found that all programs appear to have sufficient staff to supervise children, at a minimum knowing where and what the children are doing. However, none of the "higher-quality" programs routinely exceeded a child-to-staff ratio of 15:1 whereas three of the five poorest-quality programs reported 20:1 ratios. It was observed that lower-quality programs may not have had enough staff at all times to provide a choice of activities, respond to individual children's concerns, and engage in activities and conversation with small groups or individual children.

Total Enrollment. Lower total enrollment is believed to allow more one-on-one time between children and staff and hence foster a more positive emotional climate and a better educational environment (if education is an objective of the program) (U.S. Departments of Education and Justice, 2000). If total enrollments are too large and supervision sporadic, safety may be an issue if staff size is not correspondingly large. Also, after-school programs (particularly school-based programs) usually rely on a single indoor space donated by another organization; under this circumstance, total enrollment influences crowding and noise indoors. There appears to be a general consensus among reports that total enrollment should be restricted to 30 children aged six and older (National Association of Elementary School Principals, 1999; U.S. Departments of Education and Justice, 2000; National School-Age Care Alliance, 1998).

The meta-analysis yields moderate support for limiting total enrollment as a practice. One Tier 1 study, four Tier 2 reports, and one Tier 3 publication suggest that total enrollment should be a practice. In one Tier 1 study, total enrollment in a program was negatively correlated with children's perceptions of the overall climate, emotional support, and autonomy/privacy of a program (Rosenthal and Vandell, 1996), consistent with the interpretation that limiting total enrollment results in better child outcomes. In a national sample of before- and after-school programs (RMC Corporation, 1993), programs with lower-quality ratings were perceived by outside observers to have unmanageable total enrollments, which gave the impression that children were crowded and precluded from developing a relationship with an adult staff member.

Mixing of Age Groups. Schools provide little opportunity for interaction with other age groups—a shortcoming that after-school programs can address (Alexander, 1986). Mixing of different age groups within after-school programs is thought to benefit older children by fostering initiative, responsibility, nurturing, cooperation, and respect for others through mentoring (Alexander, 1986; National Research Council and Institute of Medicine, 2000). In addition, younger children and adolescents may be provided with an opportunity to master a range of different skills and abilities (National Research Council and Institute of Medicine, 2000).

The meta-analysis yields moderate support for age-group mixing as a practice. One Tier 1 and one Tier 3 study find a positive relationship between mixing of age groups and the quality of an after-school program. In the Tier 1 study, programs with a smaller proportion of older children (and hence less age-group mixing) had a greater frequency of observed negative staff-child interactions (Rosenthal and Vandell, 1996). In the Tier 3 study (involving an evaluation of two pilot programs), principals and staff perceived that mixing age groups in before- and after-school care led to improved relationships among students of different ages and aided the children's personal growth and social development by teaching them how to work in groups. Older children gained a sense of responsibility while acting as positive role models for the younger children (Finn-Stevenson, Desimone, and Chung, 1998). This practice is further supported by two Tier 2 and one Tier 4 study.

Age-Appropriate Activities. The lack of age-appropriate activities is believed to contribute to higher student dropout rates, particularly of older children (in fourth grade and higher) in after-school programs (RMC Corporation, 1993). Examples of age-appropriate activities for older children, which many after-school programs lack, include participation in community activities, opportunities to perform community service, and career exploration (RMC Corporation, 1993). Several Tier 2 publications recommend that after-school care activities, in addition to being age-appropriate, be challenging, reflect the different interests of children, and represent a range of choices (National Research Council and Institute of Medicine, 2000; U.S. Departments of Education and Justice, 2000; National School-Age Care Alliance, 1998). Only 51 percent of the programs that serve children in fourth grade and above provide activities for these older children that differ from the activities for the younger children (RMC Corporation, 1993).

The meta-analysis provides moderate support for the provision of age-appropriate activities as a practice. A Tier 3 national study of before- and after-school programs (RMC Corporation, 1993) concluded that programs that were assessed as high quality are more likely to provide age-appropriate activities for older children than lower-quality programs. In addition, six Tier 2 publications recommend age-appropriate activities.

Space and Furnishings Available. A commonly mentioned practice is the provision of sufficient indoor and outdoor space for activities. Sufficient space can lead to a wider array of activities (including physically active games), room for expansion, storage space for equipment and supplies, and less crowding of children. One factor frequently mentioned as a potentially negative influence on space availability is whether a program must share space.

The meta-analysis yields moderate support of space availability as a practice, with seven Tier 2 publications providing recommendations regarding space. Panels suggested not only that there should be ample space for both indoor and outdoor activities (U.S. Departments of Education and Justice, 2000; National Association of Elementary School Principals, 1999) but that the physical space available should be used effectively (National Research Council and Institute of Medicine, 2000) and be safe and designed to meet the physical, emotional, and social needs of the children (Miller and Marx, 1990). Two Tier 3 studies also support this practice. In a Tier 3 study, programs with higher-quality rankings were more likely to have access to dedicated primary program space (usually a classroom) and arranged their quiet and interest-area activity spaces to be inviting and homelike. Programs with lower assessed quality tended to have insufficient room for children to pursue activities without crowding, and children were less likely to be engaged in helping keep their space clean or involved in decorating their space (RMC Corporation, 1993).

Continuity and Complementarity with Day School Programs. Continuity and complementarity with day school teachers (referring specifically to collaboration on curriculum and sharing information about student progress) is moderately supported as a practice. Continuity and complementarity are most relevant for school-based after-school programs, particularly those with a focus on improving academic achievement. The notion behind this practice is to integrate after-school time with the traditional school day and to forge sound relationships between the school and after-school care center (Walter, Caplan, and McElvain, 2000) in an effort to keep children interested in learning. The National Association of Elementary School Principals (1999) recommends that programs appoint a program director responsible for maintaining coordination with the day school and with facilitating the sharing of information on day-school curriculum, homework assignments, assessment results, and instructional strategies (National Association of Elementary School Principals, 1999).

Eight Tier 2 studies support this practice. An emphasis of the Tier 2 publications is on supporting a true partnership between the day school and after-school care programs (U.S. Departments of Education and Justice, 2000). Advantages to this are multiple; for example, it may increase staff morale (Baden et al., 1982) thereby decreasing turnover and improving the emotional climate, and it may build in a mechanism for staff to receive informal training from teachers. This training can be built in by setting aside time for staff and teachers to communicate on a regular basis (Baden et al., 1982), including having after-school care staff attend faculty meetings and coordinate their work with classroom teachers.

Four Tier 3 studies also support the importance of continuity and complementarity with day school programs. In one study, staff in two pilot programs observed that day school teachers did not support the programs and that the program and classrooms were viewed as two separate entities unable to work together. Observers remarked that this might have been due to teachers' exclusion from the initial planning process for the pilot programs. During the next two years of the evaluation, efforts were made to improve communication with teachers and to increase teacher involvement in the program. As a result, relations between staff and teachers greatly improved. Staff reported that they discussed particular students with teachers and collaborated to meet the needs of these children, which the staff viewed as productive and helpful (Finn-Stevenson, Desimone, and Chung, 1998).

Clear Goals and Evaluation of Program Progress and Effectiveness. A practice that receives much attention in the literature is establishing clear goals and continuous evaluation of program progress and effectiveness. Although this practice has its roots in the accreditation process, setting goals and performing ongoing evaluations is widely believed to be a practice that quality programs follow even when accreditation is not an issue. Most before- and after-school programs (83 percent) nationally undertake a formal review or evaluation at least annually (RMC Corporation, 1993).

The meta-analysis provides moderate support for clear goals and evaluations as a practice. Nine Tier 2 studies and one Tier 3 publication recommend goal setting and ongoing program evaluation as an indicator of center quality, with at least two of these reports noting that continuous program evaluation and improvement are crucial to effective program implementation (National Association of Elementary School Principals, 1999; Fashola, 1998). To effectively evaluate a program's success, it is recommended that programs clearly state their intended goals and desired outcomes (National Research Council and Institute of Medicine, 2000; U.S. Departments of Education and Justice, 2000).

Most studies agree that program goals should be jointly established by community leaders, program staff, parents (and youth), and community members (National School-Age Care Alliance, 1998; National Institute on Out-of-School Time, 2000). Recommendations about continuous evaluations are more complex. One of the more basic approaches to assessing the degree to which a program is achieving some measure of success is to poll young people, families, and staff to see if their needs are adequately served (National Research Council and Institute of Medicine, 2000). At least one expert questions whether these informal methodologies are designed well enough to determine if the programs achieve desired outcomes (Fashola, 1998). One of the more effective approaches involves a stronger research design, such as assessing the performance of students in an after-school program compared to a control group or comparison group in the district (Fashola, 1998; U.S. Departments of Education and Justice, 2000). The more comprehensive approaches focus on data collection efforts that allow measurement of progress toward meeting program goals (U.S. Departments of Education and Justice, 2000).

Materials. An ample supply of materials and well-maintained equipment receives moderate support as a practice in the meta-analysis. An adequate supply of materials and equipment ensures choice of activities (National School-Age Care Alliance, 1998) and decreases the chance of conflict both among participants and between the program and other programs or institutions (if a program is operating in a shared environment). One of the most common complaints about after-school programs is the lack of coordination regarding equipment such as sports supplies and computers (U.S. Departments of Education and Justice, 2000).

Six Tier 2 publications and two Tier 3 studies emphasize the importance of maintaining an adequate supply of materials. Two reports emphasize that materials should be in good repair to decrease the risk of accidents (National Association of Elementary School Principals, 1999; National School-Age Care Alliance, 1998). In the RMC Corporation (1993) study, lower-quality programs reported insufficient supplies, equipment, and materials and observed that children were more likely to argue over the use of the equipment.

Attention to Safety and Health. Attention to safety and health receives moderate support in the meta-analysis. This practice generally refers to the safety of the physical environment, personal hygiene, and the nutritional needs of children while in the program. The provision of nutritious snacks and other meals, when appropriate, promotes relaxation, socializing, and sound nutrition (U.S. Departments of Education and Justice, 2000; Carnegie Council on Adolescent Development, 1994).

Nine Tier 2 publications and two Tier 3 studies encourage attention to safety and health and to the general assurance that program environments foster a sense of safety and security among children (National Research Council and Institute of Medicine, 2000; U.S. Departments of Education and Justice, 2000; National School-Age Care Alliance, 1998; Miller and Marx, 1990; National Association of Elementary School Principals, 1999). One Tier 2 study suggests the placement of systems to monitor and ensure the safety of the facility and equipment (National Association of Elementary School Principals, 1999). More specific recommendations related to safety include requiring children to sign into and out of centers and providing first aid training to staff (National Institute on Out-of-School Time, 2000; National Association of Elementary School Principals, 1999; National School-Age Care Alliance, 1998).

Recommendations about attention to the health of students focus on the provision of nutritious snacks or meals (U.S. Departments of Education and Justice, 2000; Miller and Marx, 1990; National Association of Elementary School Principals, 1999; National Institute on Out-of-School Time, 2000; Carnegie Council on Adolescent Development, 1994; National School-Age Care Alliance, 1998), particularly foods that are low in fat and sugar (National Association of Elementary School Principals, 1999).

In some states, health and safety considerations are the only requirements state child care licensing agencies have for program licensure. This could partially explain its inclusion in a relatively high number of Tier 2 publications.

Community Contacts

Involvement of Families. The meta-analysis provides a moderate level of support for the involvement of families in programs as a practice. Family involvement can increase the pool of volunteers available to assist staff and improve fundraising. Family involvement also ensures that parents' and children's program expectations are incorporated into objective formulation and that their perceptions are considered in the evaluation process (Fashola, 1998). In a national sample of before- and after-school programs, 11 percent of programs interviewed required that parents become involved in some aspect of the program, and 36 percent reported that parents serve on the board of directors or some other advisory group. More than half (62 percent) of the programs indicated that parents are involved in planning activities and evaluation, with a large proportion of programs involving parents in other ways, such as volunteering, fundraising, and attending parent meetings (RMC Corporation, 1993).

Ten Tier 2 publications and one Tier 3 study emphasize the benefits derived from family involvement in after-school care programs, including maintenance of strong lines of communication between parents and programs (National Research Council and Institute of Medicine, 2000; National Association of Elementary School Principals, 1999; National School-Age Care Alliance, 1998; Miller and Marx, 1990); parent input regarding program policies and procedures (National Association of Elementary School Principals, 1999), and child and parent involvement to ensure that the program captures children's interests and ultimately produces lower dropout rates (Fashola, 1998; U.S. Departments of Education and Justice, 2000).

In the RMC Corporation (1993) study, programs that were ranked as being of lower quality reported fewer staff-parent conversations regarding the children; on the other hand, better-quality programs reported more such conversations than the average program and were more likely to invite parents to serve on advisory councils and the board of directors.

Use of Volunteers. The use of volunteers in programs is a practice that is moderately supported by the meta-analysis, particularly if volunteers are trained and effectively managed. Among the benefits of enlisting volunteers is the reduction in child-to-staff ratios while reducing the price of the program (U.S. Departments of Education and Justice, 2000). Four Tier 2 publications and one Tier 3 study promote the use of volunteers, who can be family members or other members of the community. One study recommends that volunteers be recruited through links with local colleges and universities and that efforts be made to seek supplementary financial or material support from parents, businesses, civic organizations, and government agencies to bolster the programs in place (National Association of Elementary School Principals, 1999). The U.S. Departments of Education and Justice (2000) recommend that volunteers receive orientation and ongoing training, much like paid staff.

Partnerships with Community-Based Organizations, Juvenile Justice Agencies, Law Enforcement, and Youth Groups. A commonly mentioned practice is partnering with community-based organizations such as youth groups and law enforcement agencies. This practice receives a moderate level of support from eight Tier 2 publications. Among the cited advantages of partnerships are student opportunities to obtain educational experience in their localities and additional resources (National Research Council and Institute of Medicine, 2000; National School-Age Care Alliance, 1998; Miller and Marx, 1990; Carnegie Council on Adolescent Development, 1994; National Institute on Out-of-School Time, 2000). The National Institute on Out-of-School Time (2000) urges programs to invite community volunteers to host field trips to community organizations and to participate in regular celebrations of students' activities and accomplishments. The institute argues that higher-quality programs should be solidly supported by community residents and agencies and recommends that this support be built through collaboration with law enforcement agencies, service providers, community-based and civic organizations, colleges, employers, arts and cultural institutions, museums, park and recreation services, and public officials (U.S. Departments of Education and Justice, 2000). Collaboration may also lead to access to additional resources, such as funding, facilities, mentors, tutors, learning experiences, and job observation experiences (U.S. Departments of Education and Justice, 2000).

Other Practices

For completeness, this category includes a sampling of practices that have been mentioned in the after-school care literature but have not received much attention. Consequently, none of these practices are rated. Some of these practices are likely to receive greater attention in the near future (e.g., culturally competent staff, outreach to diverse groups) and are worth heeding as the body of literature on after-school programs develops. They are as follows:

- Tutoring (Morris, Shaw, and Perney, 1990)

- Self-help skills, which include skills necessary for daily living, such as sewing a button, scrambling an egg, and other tasks that busy working parents may not have the time, energy, or patience to do (Alexander, 1986)

- A nonsexist approach (Alexander, 1986)

- Limiting and supervising use of television (Alexander, 1986)

- Emphasizing cooperation, not competition (Alexander, 1986)

- A solid organizational structure, which includes hands-on, site-based management with regular oversight and accountability to all partners (U.S. Departments of Education and Justice, 2000)

- Effective management and sustainability (U.S. Departments of Education and Justice, 2000)

- Compliance with legal requirements (U.S. Departments of Education and Justice, 2000)

- Effective program administration (U.S. Departments of Education and Justice, 2000)

- A culturally competent staff (National Research Council and Institute of Medicine, 2000)

- Outreach to diverse groups of children and adolescents (National Research Council and Institute of Medicine, 2000)

- The conduct of background checks on all staff and volunteers (National Institute on Out-of-School Time, 2000)

- Individual assessment and "tracking" of children's participation and progress (Halpern, 1991)

- Use of recognition strategies that focus on the achievements of children, e.g., publishing a quarterly newsletter that focuses on the achievements of children in school and at the after-school program (Halpern, 1991)

- Establishing the legal status of the organization (nonprofit, for-profit) (Kisker et al., 1991)

- Establishment of an advisory board (Fashola, 1998)

- Accreditation (Whitebrook, Howes, and Phillips, 1989; Whitebrook, Phillips, and Howes, 1993; Cost, Quality, and Outcomes Study Team, 1995).

SUMMARY OF LITERATURE REVIEW

Our meta-analysis of after-school care literature initially identified 20 indicators of quality after-school care or practices based on our assessment of a composite of published empirical research, evaluations of individual after-school programs, reports produced by expert panels or professional organizations, and other single-authored articles or reports. In order to evaluate the quality of this literature, we classified publications by type of publication or author, assessed the quality of each type, and then derived an empirical measure of the strength of support for a particular practice across the publication types.

We identified three levels of support for each practice. Three practices (variety of activities, flexibility of programming, and emotional climate) received strong support based on our meta-analysis; fifteen practices were moderately supported by the literature; and two practices (turnover rate and staff experience) received limited support. Because of the limited support provided by the literature for turnover rate and staff experience, our final list of recommended practices based on the meta-analysis excludes these two indicators, leaving a final tally of 18 indicators. As the after-school care literature develops in the coming years, one or both of the practices that received limited support may emerge as moderately (or even strongly) supported in the literature; however, given the current state of knowledge, we are least confident in these practices as indicators of quality after-school care.

Chapter Three summarizes our approach toward measuring the adherence of a sample of after-school programs to each of these 18 practices.

MEASURING ADHERENCE TO AFTER-SCHOOL CARE PRACTICES

In this chapter, we describe how we measured adherence to the after-school practices identified in the previous chapter for our sponsor, Stone Soup Child Care Programs.

Stone Soup Child Care Programs is a nonprofit organization supported by contributions from foundations, corporations and local businesses, government, and individuals. Stone Soup provides after-school programs in low-income communities in California. The stated objective of Stone Soup is to ensure "quality child care for school-age children that is safe, dependable, and affordable through a managed program of shared resources and goals." Since its inception in 1987, enrollment in Stone Soup after-school programs has grown to 3,500 children. Generally, each Stone Soup program partners with the local school district, parents, and sometimes the local government. The school district provides space, utilities, custodial and payroll services, and liability insurance. Local government agencies may provide park sites, in-kind donations, and financial support for tuition. Parents pay a low monthly fee—$83 for one child in 1999 (according to Stone Soup, this figure is about one-third to one-half the cost for comparable programs in the same communities it serves).[1] Stone Soup develops programs; recruits, trains, and supervises staff; manages day-to-day operations; and raises money from private sources to supplement revenue from parents.

_____

[1]Information provided by Stone Soup.

Most Stone Soup programs operate in K–5 schools, with about one-half of the students served in kindergarten to second grades, one-third of students in the third through fifth grades, and the remainder in grades six through eight. Currently, Stone Soup operates 72 programs in 16 school districts throughout urban and rural California. After-school care begins at the end of the school day and ends at 6:30 p.m. In addition to after-school care, Stone Soup offers before-school care, kindergarten care, and full-day care during summer vacation and other days when children are not in school.

Stone Soup sought to evaluate how well the program is achieving its objectives. The "safe and affordable" components of the primary objective can be gauged through straightforward means, such as polling parents. On an annual basis, Stone Soup conducts a self-evaluation that includes eliciting parent and child feedback to ensure that they are meeting goals, such as being safe and affordable. Stone Soup recognized, however, that the "quality care" component is more difficult to measure because it can be subjective and requires a thorough assessment of the relevant literature; thus, it asked RAND to conduct an independent assessment.

In the context of a modest budget and time constraints, we sought the most cost-effective and time-efficient approach toward developing and implementing a study design to measure adherence to practices for the Stone Soup programs. It was immediately obvious that we would be able to measure adherence only to a subset or sample of programs, since in order to understand the context of these programs, we wanted to conduct site visits to all of the programs we evaluated. We thus drew a stratified random sample (as described in the next subsection) so that we could draw inferences about how well the full set of Stone Soup programs adhere to the 18 practices. To the extent possible, we designed a survey instrument that incorporated already-developed and -tested survey and observational instruments to measure each of the practices. When we were unable to identify measures for a particular practice in the published literature, we wrote new survey questions. These questions were used to develop rating scales to measure the degree of adherence to each practice. Each of these steps is detailed below. The instruments we developed are given in Appendix C.

SAMPLE SELECTION AND STUDY PROTOCOL

In order to ensure that the programs evaluated were representative of the Stone Soup program throughout California in terms of geography, student body racial/ethnic composition, socioeconomic status (SES), and other characteristics, we elected to use stratified random selection of campuses. On the basis of the budget available for site visits, we selected 10 programs from a frame of programs in 67 sites by means of proportionate stratified random sampling. (The small sample size means that the inferences we make to the larger population are unbiased but imprecise.)[2] Using information on student enrollment by district provided by Stone Soup, six strata were defined as follows:

- **Southern California:** lower-SES districts with a Hispanic majority (33 sites)

- **Southern California:** higher-SES districts with a Hispanic majority (10 sites)

- **Central Valley:** districts with a non-Hispanic white majority (4 sites)

- **Central Valley:** districts without a non-Hispanic white majority (8 sites)

- **Monterrey County:** higher-SES districts with a non-Hispanic white plurality (10 sites)

- **Monterrey County:** lower-SES districts with a Hispanic majority (two sites).

Four sites were selected from the first stratum, two from the second stratum, and one each from the four remaining strata. In addition, we conducted pretests at two additional programs. The pilot programs were selected because they were large and located in Los Angeles. The results presented in this report are based on the ten randomly selected programs.

---

[2]Ideally, one would want to visit a larger number of sites to obtain a more reliable estimate of the overall adherence of Stone Soup programs to the practices.

INSTRUMENT DEVELOPMENT

The first step in instrument development involved scanning the after-school care literature to identify instruments other researchers or administrators have used to measure adherence to each of the 18 practices. To accomplish this task, we undertook an extensive review of the research studies and materials developed by committees. We restricted our search for extant survey questions to items that have been published, tested, and successfully implemented. Sources for our items are the School-Age Care Environment Scale, or SACERS, and items used by Rosenthal and Vandell (1996), Walter, Caplan, and McElvain (2000), and the RMC Corporation (1993) in its *National Study of Before- and After-School Programs*. SACERS was developed as a comprehensive rating scale for school-age child care programs and is based on similar instruments developed for early childhood care assessment. It is a combination observational and interview instrument that assesses six aspects of after-school programs: Space and Furnishings, Health and Safety, Activities, Interactions, Program Structure, and Staff Development (Harms, Jacobs, and White, 1996). Because these subscales in many cases combined more than one of the practices we sought to measure, we restricted their use to those instances where a subscale mapped to a single practice (e.g., the Health and Safety subscale was used to assess the Attention to Safety and Health practice). Combined, these sources provided us with the information we needed for about half of the practices. For the remaining practices, we wrote our own questions. We developed two survey instruments that incorporate these questions.

The final set of instruments we used consisted of two instruments we developed and a third preexisting instrument. The first instrument we developed (the Stone Soup Survey) is a questionnaire designed to elicit administrative information (total enrollment, staffing, wages, and training staff) for each site from Stone Soup headquarters. The second instrument we developed, the Site Supervisor Survey, elicited information on the operations of each site (e.g., the variety of activities offered, mixing of age groups, space availability, and use of volunteers). It was sent to each site supervisor.[3] The third instrument

---

[3]We met with Stone Soup's board of directors and president to identify those questions that could be obtained directly from Stone Soup's administrative records and

we used was the already-developed SACERS.   An experienced methodologist from the RAND Survey Research Group reviewed the formatting and wording of the Stone Soup and Site Supervisor surveys to ensure face validity and coherence.   Prior to the full-scale data collection effort, we piloted all three instruments at one school. We probed the individuals who completed the surveys to ensure that there was no confusion or ambiguity in the two instruments we developed as well as to ensure that the surveys were sufficiently short. (Appendix C contains the Stone Soup and Site Supervisor survey instruments.) The pilot was also important for ensuring that the three authors of this report, who also served as observers for the SACERS component of the data collection effort, recorded similar responses to the SACERS items. In the few cases where one of us differed from the other two observers, we discussed the discrepancies and reached a consensus about the proper coding of the items before conducting the site visits.

LIMITATION OF OUR SURVEY INSTRUMENTS

One major limitation of our assessment of Stone Soup after-school care programs was that we did not collect information from all the major stakeholders (i.e., teachers, principals, parents, and children). The most comprehensive assessment to our knowledge, carried out by Vandell and associates (e.g., Vandell and Pierce, 2001; Rosenthal and Vandell, 1996), collected information from parents and students as well as an assessment by an outside observer of program operations. Vandell and Pierce used observer ratings on SACERS, observer qualitative ratings of children's program experiences, children's reports on their experiences, and mothers' reports about the programs. The observer qualitative ratings are a combination of ratings used by Rosenthal and Vandell and the Observational Record of the Caregiving Environment by the National Institute of Child Health and Human Development (NICHD) Study of Early Child Care. The children reported on their experiences, such as emotional support from staff and autonomy and privacy, while parents reported on perceptions about physical setting, program activities, and the like. Impor-

---

those questions that were more appropriately asked of the site supervisors. The Stone Soup board was further asked to identify which employee at the program level (i.e., the site supervisor) would be the most appropriate person for answering the survey.

tantly, children's reports on their experiences in the programs were more strongly linked to child outcomes (loneliness and depression) than were parent reports or observer ratings. Parents' perceptions may be important because ultimately they decide if a child will remain in a formal after-school program or move either to another formal care setting or to an informal setting (Rosenthal and Vandell, 1996). Thus, we recognize that a more comprehensive data collection would include child and parent reports.[4]

DATA COLLECTION PROTOCOL AND SITE VISITS

The protocol for data collection and site visits to the ten randomly selected programs was as follows. The president of Stone Soup Foundation and the Stone Soup board members served as intermediaries between RAND, the schools, and the after-school programs in setting up the site visits and faxing the Site Supervisor Surveys. Prior to the first site visit, RAND sent the Stone Soup Survey instrument to the Stone Soup central office to obtain information available from the central office. (In designing the survey instruments, we consulted with the president and the board regarding which information they could provide from their administrative records.) About a week before a site visit, the Stone Soup central office faxed the Site Supervisor Survey to site supervisors. Site supervisors were asked to complete the survey instrument and to return it directly to the RAND researcher at the beginning of the site visit to ensure confidentiality. The primary objective of the site visit (by one of the authors) was to administer the SACERS instrument, developed by early-childhood researchers and practitioners in North America to assess the quality of programs for school-age children (Harms, Jacobs, and White, 1996). The site visits generally started at 2 p.m. and ended at 5 p.m. All site visits were completed in March 2001.

---

[4]The collection of information from parents and students was not feasible given our time constraints (approximately four months to develop the instrument and collect all the data). Because the programs we evaluated were school-based, in addition to a more time- and resource-intensive internal human subjects review process, we would have needed to obtain approval from each school district's superintendent, each school's principal, and parents.

RATING SCALES

With the exception of the four SACERS items we used, we derived the rating scales for all items discussed in this section on the basis of our reading of the literature on after-school care practices. Whenever possible, we sought guidance from existing standards or state averages to devise scales. In most cases, however, there was a paucity of such guidance. Except where noted, we derived our own scales on the basis of our reading of the literature.

We sought to develop a consistent rating scale across practices that reflected degree of adherence. Since the SACERS instrument had already been validated extensively and since we used several of the SACERS subscales and individual items in our instrument, we borrowed the SACERS scale and labeling system. Scoring for each of the items and subscales on SACERS can be rounded off to a four-point system: excellent, good, minimal, and inadequate. In SACERS, "excellent" describes high-quality care that enhances children's experiences, extends their learning, and provides warm and caring support. A "good" rating indicates the basic dimensions of developmentally appropriate care. A "minimal" rating describes custodial-level care. Finally, a rating of "inadequate" represents a lack of care that compromises children's development. Our coding of the four-point scale by practice follows.

Training Staff. Compliance with this practice was measured using the Stone Soup Central Survey (questions 6 and 10) about the particular types of training the site supervisor and the assistant with the longest tenure had received in the past year. The percentage of training items completed (regardless of who paid for the training) was calculated. The site supervisor percentage score was based on a checklist of 17 items, while the assistant's score was based on 13. The site supervisor's training score was based on an additional four topics (budgeting/financial management, data collection, program evaluation, and administration) that are appropriate to a managerial position but not to nonmanagerial staff. The final code was assessed based on the average of the site supervisor's and the assistant's scores. The qualitative code assigned to a score was based on a standard "grading system" (A or excellent = 90 percent or higher, B or good = 80 percent to 89 percent, and so on).

Code	Rating Scale
Excellent	Average percentage score $\geq$ 90 percent
Good	80 percent $\leq$ average percentage score < 90 percent
Minimal	70 percent $\leq$ average percentage score < 80 percent
Inadequate	Average percentage score < 70 percent

Staff Education. Compliance with this practice was based on the highest level of education completed by the site supervisor at a particular site.[5]

Code	Rating Scale
Excellent	Bachelor's degree or higher
Good	Associate degree
Minimal	High school diploma, General Equivalency Diploma (GED), some college, or child development associate training
Inadequate	No high school diploma

Staff Compensation. Compliance with this practice was measured using the hourly wages paid as reported in the Stone Soup Central Survey (questions 7 and 11). We calculated the average hourly wage paid for each program on the basis of the hourly wage paid to the supervisor and the hourly wage paid to assistants. The average hourly wage paid at the site was compared to the average hourly wages paid to child care workers in the county where the program is located.[6] The county-level wages are from the 1998 *California Occupational Employment Statistics Survey*. A cost-of-living adjustment was applied to the 1998 values to reflect current wages.

---

[5]When we designed the data collection instrument, we assumed that the site supervisors would have had the highest level of education of all the staff. During our site visits, however, we observed that several sites had one or two assistants who had higher levels of education than the site supervisors (i.e., the assistants were college students with an interest in child development). In retrospect, we would have collected information about all staff at a site and calculated the modal level of education. In this instance, we anticipate that the modal education would have been the same as the site supervisor's education.

[6]Because data collected on wages for assistants are based on the assistant with the longest tenure at Stone Soup, this measure will slightly inflate the calculated average wage for site supervisor and assistant. However, we were told that the wages for assistants are not highly differentiated by tenure.

Code	Rating Scale
Excellent	Hourly wage paid ≥ 75th percentile of hourly child care worker wage in county
Good	Median wage ≤ hourly wage paid < 75th percentile
Minimal	25th percentile ≤ hourly wage paid < median wage
Inadequate	Hourly wage paid < 25th percentile of hourly child care worker wage in county

Variety of Activities. Compliance with this practice was measured using question 3 of the Site Supervisor Survey, which asked about the frequency of the availability of each of nine classes of activities (although we inquired about 15 specific activities). These classes of activities were weighted equally in the absence of any evidence that some activities should be weighted more heavily than others. The classes of activities (and their corresponding specific activities) are:

- Arts and crafts (item A)

- Music and movement (items N and O)

- Blocks and construction (item B)

- Physically active play (item P)

- Drama/theater (items L and M)

- Language/reading (items E and F)

- Homework time (item G)

- Math/reasoning (item D)

- Science/nature activities (item C)

Each program was scored the basis of the number of activities offered and the frequency of offerings (similar to the approach used by Rosenthal and Vandell, 1996). An activity offered daily or weekly was allocated a weight of 1, while an activity offered monthly was allocated a weight of 0.25. Activities that were not offered at least monthly were given zero weight. The Variety of Activities score was calculated by taking an average across all activities for each program. A score of 1 on this measure indicates that a program offers each class of activity daily or weekly; a score of 0 indicates that none of the classes of activities are offered weekly or monthly. The cutoff points were established by modifying the standard grading system such that

> 85% = A (or excellent). Lowering the threshold permits a program that offers on a weekly basis all but one of the types of activities to attain an "excellent" rating.

Code	Rating Scale
Excellent	Activities score > 0.85
Good	$0.70 <$ activities score ≤ 0.85
Minimal	$0.60 \leq$ activities score ≤ 0.70
Inadequate	Activities score < 0.60

Flexibility of Programming. Compliance with this practice was measured on the basis of an item from SACERS related to children's flexibility in selecting materials and companions and, as far as possible, to play independently.

Code	Rating Scale
Excellent	SACERS score $= 7$
Good	$5 \leq$ SACERS score < 7
Minimal	$3 \leq$ SACERS score < 5
Inadequate	SACERS score < 3

Emotional Climate. Measurement of this practice was based on the average of a program's score across items in the Interactions subscale of SACERS. Interactions include measures of staff-child, staff-staff, staff-faculty, staff-parent, and child-child interactions.

Code	Rating Scale
Excellent	Average SACERS score $= 7$
Good	$5 \leq$ average SACERS score < 7
Minimal	$3 \leq$ average SACERS score < 5
Inadequate	Average SACERS score < 3

Child-to-Staff Ratio. Compliance with this practice was measured using afternoon enrollment as reported in the Stone Soup Central Survey and the average number of paid after-school care staff that have direct contact with these children as reported in question 33 of the Site Supervisor Survey. The ratio of these two values was taken.

Code	Rating Scale
Excellent	Ratio ≤ 9:1
Good	9:1 < ratio ≤ 12:1
Minimal	12:1 < ratio ≤ 15:1[7]
Inadequate	Ratio > 15:1

Total Enrollment. Compliance with this practice was measured using question 1 of the Stone Soup Central Survey to determine the total enrollment of children in the program.

Code	Rating Scale
Excellent	Total enrollment < 30
Good	30 ≤ total enrollment < 45
Minimal	45 ≤ total enrollment ≤ 60
Inadequate	Total enrollment > 60

Mixing of Age Groups. Compliance with this practice was measured using question 2 of the Stone Soup Central Survey and questions 5 and 6 of the Site Supervisor Survey. The percentage of students in grade three and higher was calculated and compared to the California average for after-school programs (22 percent). Unlike other scales, we calculated this score in relation to the state average because it is available. In addition, we took into account the extent of interaction reported between older and younger children.

Code	Rating Scale
Excellent	Percentage older children ≥ California average and Q 5 = yes and Q 6 = yes
Good	Percentage older children ≥ California average and Q 5 and/or Q 6 = no
Minimal	Percentage older children < California average and Q 5 = yes and Q 6 = yes

---

[7]Our threshold for meeting the "minimal" requirement for child development will differ from that used in regulations. For example, the California Department of Social Services Child Care Center general licensing requirements stipulate at least one instructor per 14 children aged six and over—a stricter requirement than our ratio of 15 children to one adult ratio (http://www.dss.cahwnet.gov/getinfo/pdf/ccc7.PDF).

Inadequate   Percentage older children < California average and
Q 5 and/or Q 6 = no

Age-Appropriate Activities. Compliance with this practice was measured on the basis of question 4 of the Site Supervisor Survey, which asks about the total number of special provisions made for children in the program over nine years old.

Code	Rating Scale
Excellent	Special provisions > 5
Good	$3 <$ special provisions ≤ 5
Minimal	$1 <$ special provisions ≤ 3
Inadequate	Special provisions ≤ 1

Space and Furnishings Available. Compliance with this practice was based on the average of a program's score across items in the Space and Furnishings subscale of SACERS. Items included in this subscale tap dimensions such as the sufficiency and nature of indoor and outdoor space, room arrangements, and the availability and condition of furnishings.

Code	Rating Scale
Excellent	Average SACERS score = 7
Good	$5 \leq$ average SACERS score < 7
Minimal	$3 \leq$ average SACERS score < 5
Inadequate	Average SACERS score < 3

Continuity and Complementarity with Day School Programs. Compliance with this practice was measured using items about staff attendance at regular school faculty meetings and communication with day school faculty about students' achievement/behavior and lesson plans/activities (questions 18–21 of the Site Supervisor Survey).

Code	Rating Scale
Excellent	Staff frequently or always attend school faculty meetings and communicate about achievement/ behavior and lesson plans/activities (Q 18 = yes and

	Q 19 = frequently or always and Q 20 = yes and Q 21 = yes)
Good	Staff rarely or occasionally attend school faculty meetings and communicate with faculty about achievement/behavior and lesson plans/activities (Q 18 = yes and Q 19 = rarely or occasionally and Q 20 = yes and Q 21 = yes)
Minimal	Staff do not attend faculty school meetings but do communicate with faculty about student achievement/behavior or lesson plans/activities (Q 18 = no and [Q 20 = yes or Q 21 = yes])
Inadequate	Staff do not attend faculty meetings and do not communicate with faculty about student achievement/behavior or lesson plans/activities (Q 18 = no and Q 20 = no and Q 21 = no)

Clear Goals and Evaluation of Program Progress and Effectiveness. Compliance with this practice was measured on the basis of items related to annual evaluation of the program, type of evaluation (formal, informal, or both), and who reviews the program (questions 39–41 of the Site Supervisor Survey).

Code	**Rating Scale**
Excellent	Annual informal and formal evaluation by program staff, parents, and at least one of following (national organization staff, funding organization staff, board of education/school district, other) (Q 39 = yes and Q 40 = informal and formal and Q 41 = program staff, parents, and at least one of three other options)
Good	Annual informal and formal evaluation by program staff and parents (Q 39 = yes and Q 40 = informal and formal and Q 41 = program staff and parents)
Minimal	Annual formal evaluation by at least two of the following (staff, parents, national organization staff, funding organization staff, board of education/school district, other) (Q 39 = yes and Q 40 = formal and Q 41 = at least two of five options)
Inadequate	None of the above

Materials. Compliance with this practice was measured using the three questions about the condition of materials and equipment children use and the availability of sufficient age-appropriate equipment for all children (questions 7–9 of the Site Supervisor Survey).

Code	Rating Scale
Excellent	The materials and equipment used by children are in excellent condition, most of the games and toys are not missing pieces, and there is sufficient age-appropriate equipment (Q 7 = excellent and Q 8 = no and Q 9 = yes)
Good	The materials and equipment used by children are in good or fair condition, most of the games and toys are not missing pieces, and there is sufficient age-appropriate equipment (Q 7 = fair or good and Q 8 = no and Q 9 = yes)
Minimal	Most of the games and toys are missing pieces or there is insufficient age-appropriate equipment (Q 8 = yes or Q 9 = no)
Inadequate	Most of the games and toys are missing pieces and there is insufficient age-appropriate equipment (Q 8 = yes and Q 9 = no)

Attention to Safety and Health. Compliance with this practice was based on the average of a program's score across items in the Health and Safety subscale of SACERS. Included are items related to health policies and practices, emergency and safety policies, and attendance protocols (e.g., what happens if a child is absent without notice).

Code	Rating Scale
Excellent	Average SACERS score = 7
Good	$5 \leq$ average SACERS score < 7
Minimal	$3 \leq$ average SACERS score < 5
Inadequate	Average SACERS score < 3

Involvement of Families. Compliance with this practice was measured using questions on parental involvement (in review process, on advisory council or board of directors, and other ways) (questions 34–38 of the Site Supervisor Survey).

Code	Rating Scale
Excellent	Parents are involved in the evaluation process, serve on the advisory committee or board of directors, and serve in least one other major way; parent involvement required (Q 34 = yes and Q 35 = yes and Q 36 = yes and Q 37 = at least one of eleven options and Q 38 = yes)
Good	Parents are involved in the evaluation process and serve in least one other major way (Q 34 = yes and Q 36 = yes and Q 37 = at least one of eleven options)
Minimal	Parents are involved in the evaluation process (Q 34 = yes)
Inadequate	Parents are not involved in the evaluation process (Q 34 = no)

Use of Volunteers. Compliance with this practice was measured using questions about programs' use of volunteers (questions 42, 44, 46–48 of the Site Supervisor Survey). Volunteers are unpaid persons who regularly visit a program. The codes reflect the extent of reliance on volunteers, ranging from a program that does not use volunteers (or if it does, a program that does not perform basic security checks or volunteer training/orientation) to one that regularly uses volunteers, has a volunteer recruiting mechanism in place, provides volunteer training and orientation, and performs background checks.

Code	Rating Scale
Excellent	Program uses volunteers, actively recruits volunteers, provides orientation or training to new volunteers, performs background checks on volunteers, and currently has at least one volunteer (Q 42 = yes and Q 44 = yes and Q 46 = yes and Q 47 = yes and Q 48 > 0)
Good	Program uses volunteers, provides orientation or training to new volunteers, performs background checks on volunteers, and currently has at least one volunteer (Q 42 = yes and Q 46 = yes and Q 47 = yes and Q 48 > 0)

| Minimal | Program uses volunteers, provides orientation or training to new volunteers, performs background checks on volunteers but currently has no volunteers; this score indicates that a program has a history of or intentions to use volunteers but currently is unsuccessful in volunteer recruiting (Q 42 = yes and Q 46 = yes and Q 47 = yes and Q 48 = 0) |
| Inadequate | Program does not use volunteers or, if the program has volunteers, does not perform background checks on volunteers or does not provide any orientation or training to volunteers; an inadequate score means that the a program does not employ volunteers or, if it does, fails to perform any security check or provide training (Q 42 = no or Q 46 = no or Q 47 = 0) |

Partnerships. Compliance with this practice was measured using items related to use of community resources and relationships with other organizations that provide community service activities for children (questions 24, 26–28 of the Site Supervisor Survey). This measure is distinct from the use of volunteers in that it indicates interaction of children in the program with community resources outside of the program.

Code	**Rating Scale**
Excellent	Program uses at least one of the listed community facilities (library, parks, community centers, swimming pool, other), partners with a community service organization in some way, and invites community members to share their resources or talents with the children at least monthly (Q 24 = yes and Q 25 = at least one of four options and Q 26 = yes and Q 27 = yes and Q 28 = weekly or monthly)
Good	Two of the following: • Program uses at least one of the listed community facilities (library, parks, community centers, swimming pool, other) (Q 24 = yes and Q 25 = at least one of four options) • Partners with a community service organization in some way (Q 26 = yes)

	• Invites community members to share their resources or talents with the children at least monthly (Q 27 = yes and Q 28 = weekly or monthly)
Minimal	Partners with a community service organization in some way or invites community members to share their resources or talents with the children (this implies a one-time visit rather than ongoing participation of a volunteer) (Q 26 = yes or Q 27 = yes)
Inadequate	None of the above

We also calculated an overall score on each practice that is the average number of points across programs. These are represented as one to four stars in the text of Chapter Four.

ADHERENCE TO AFTER-SCHOOL CARE PRACTICES BY STONE SOUP PROGRAMS: RESULTS

In this chapter, we describe how we used the information collected from the sample of Stone Soup programs to evaluate the overall adherence of the programs to the 18 practices moderately and strongly supported by the literature review in Chapter One. We also summarize some of the recommendations we made on the basis of this assessment. This section discusses how we attempted to identify characteristics of programs that adhere uniformly well or poorly to good practices. We conclude this section with a discussion of limitations we encountered in our analysis and discuss ways to overcome them in future efforts.

SUMMARY ANALYSIS

To analyze the information collected from the site visits and the Stone Soup Central and Site Supervisor surveys, we first assessed the degree to which each site adhered to each practice using the four-point rating scale outlined in Chapter Three. We wanted to identify those practices to which, on the whole, Stone Soup programs adhered closely and those practices in which there is room for improvement. To do so, we averaged the ratings across the ten sites to compute an overall rating for each practice. These ratings ranged from "excellent" to "minimal"; the programs received no "inadequate" ratings. The ratings, shown in Table 4.1, are denoted as follows: excellent = ****; good = ***; minimal = **; and inadequate = *.

Table 4.1

Summary Ratings by Practice

Practice	Summary Rating
Staff characteristics	
Training staff	****
Education	**
Compensation	***
Program characteristics	
Variety of activities	***
Flexibility of programming	***
Emotional climate	***
Child-to-staff ratio	***
Total enrollment	***
Mixing of age groups	***
Age-appropriate activities	**
Space and furnishings	***
Continuity and complementarity with day school programs	**
Clear goals and evaluation of program	***
Materials	***
Attention to safety and health	***
Community contacts	
Involvement of families	***
Use of volunteers	**
Partnerships with community-based organizations, etc.	***

Next, we broke the "good" category, which comprised most of the practices, into two parts: that for which there was little variation in ratings across sites, and that for which there was greater variation. The first part includes those practices whose adherence scores did not vary by more than one category. We were interested in finding practices to which adherence varied substantially across sites, because this variation suggested room for improvement on the part of some sites (if some sites adhered at the excellent or good level, perhaps all could).

The next subsection presents the Stone Soup results we presented for three practices. The intent of this discussion is to illustrate how to conceptualize adherence to practices across a group of programs and to illustrate the types of recommendations that can be made on the basis of this type of analysis. For the first practice, training staff, Stone Soup received an "excellent" rating. The second practice represents one in which Stone Soup did well with little variation. The third practice is one for which they received a "good" score, but with variation across programs (i.e., this is a practice on which Stone Soup has potential for improvement).

FINDINGS AND RECOMMENDATIONS

Practices for Which Stone Soup Was Rated Excellent: Training Staff

With eight out of ten programs achieving a score of "excellent," Stone Soup's overall adherence to the staff training practice was rated excellent (Figure 4.1). According to information provided by the central Stone Soup office, all of the site supervisors and those assistants with the longest tenure in the program had attended at least one Stone Soup–sponsored one-day workshop in the past year. Areas in which all or most staff received training in the past year include child abuse recognition, child development, health and nutrition, conflict resolution, classroom management, working with special needs students, multicultural awareness, gender bias avoidance, design of engaging activities, data collection, program evaluation, curriculum

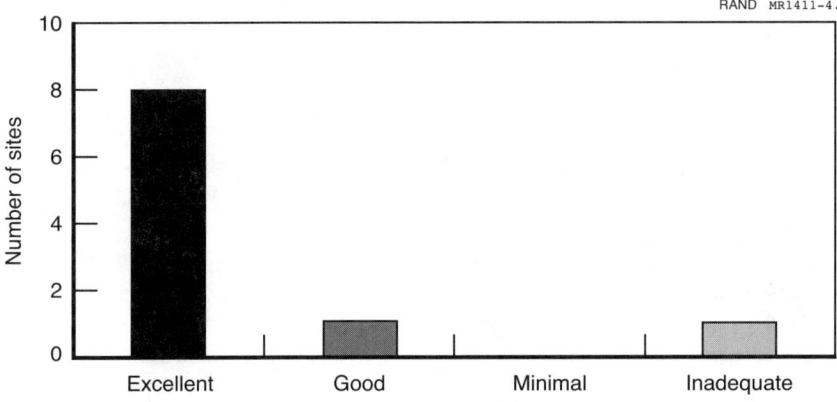

Figure 4.1—Practice: Training Staff

training, budgeting, and communication. Few site supervisors received training in administration or computer skills. The latter might receive special attention for improvement given that several sites had computers.

We collected the same information about training topics from the site supervisors themselves for two reasons. First, we wanted to identify any additional training a site supervisor may have received independent of Stone Soup; and second, the Stone Soup board was interested in learning what topics the staff thought they had covered in the workshops. The site supervisors reported more computer training than we found through the central survey. However, they reported considerably less training in gender bias avoidance, data collection, program evaluation, design of engaging activities, and communication. These differences highlight the importance of obtaining some types of information from multiple sources.

Practices for Which Stone Soup Was Rated Good, with Little Variation Across Sites: Safety and Health

Overall, Stone Soup adhered well to the safety-and-health practice criterion (Figure 4.2). Compliance with this practice was based on the Safety and Health subscale of SACERS, which included items related to health policies and practices, emergency and safety policies,

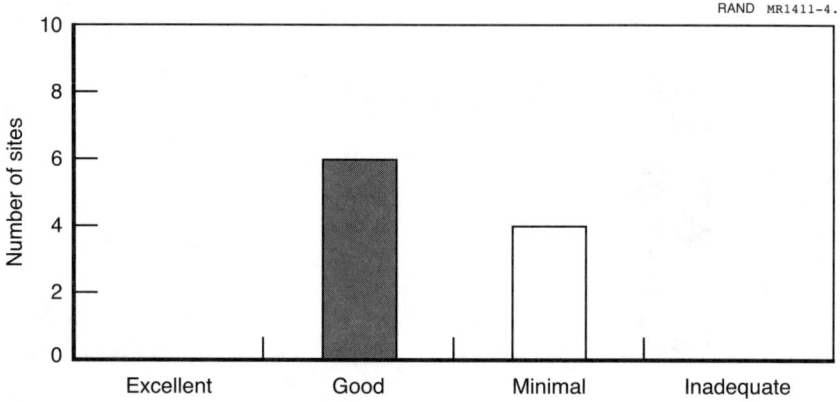

Figure 4.2—Practice: Safety and Health

attendance protocols, and personal hygiene. Stone Soup has a pre-scribed health policy about which staff and parents are well in-formed; the sites performed uniformly well on this component of the measure. The sites were observed to have a sound set of emergency and safety procedures. Both staff and children seemed well versed in the emergency procedures; however, a few programs did not have the emergency procedures posted (which should be require at all sites).

We observed a solid set of attendance protocols that were strictly ad-hered to at all sites visited. Parents were required to sign children out of the program in the afternoon before leaving, and each site had a policy of contacting either the school or the parent directly if a child was absent without notice. Adherence to safety and health was weakest with regard to personal hygiene. Many of the sites were re-quired to share bathrooms with the schools in which they were lo-cated, and these bathrooms were often unclean or lacking in basic supplies such as toilet paper, soap, and hand towels. Because the sites are school-based, the after-school program staff have limited control over the cleanliness of the bathrooms. Some site personnel have developed good relationships with the janitors who clean the bathrooms for the after-school care children and provide bathroom supplies. We recommended that Stone Soup encourage their staff to use this approach where sanitation is an issue. We further suggested that Stone Soup sites have basic bathroom supplies on hand in each of its programs for children to use if the school supplies are depleted.

Practices for Which Stone Soup Was Rated Good, with Greater Variation Across Sites: Variety of Activities

Stone Soup adhered well to the practice of providing a variety of ac-tivities (Figure 4.3). To receive a "good" rating, a program had to of-fer seven (of nine) categories of activities at least weekly (an "excellent" score was assigned to the three sites that on average of-fered at least eight of the nine activities on a weekly basis). Compli-ance with this practice was based on the site supervisor's account of activities offered. The results indicate that there is room for im-provement at some sites.

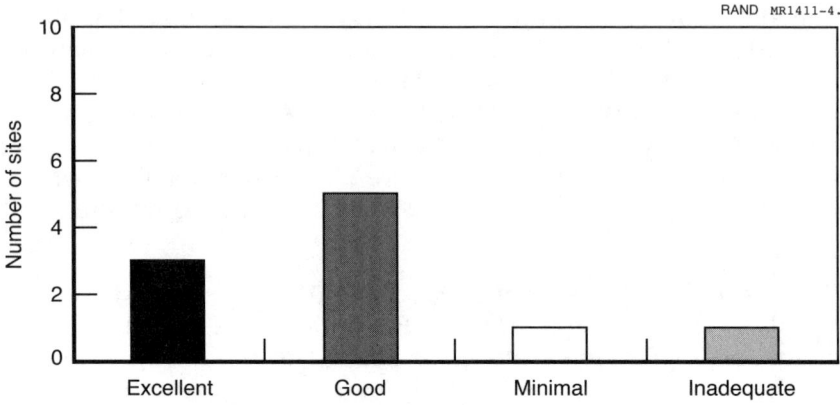

RAND MR1411-4.

Figure 4.3—Practice: Variety of Activities

However, we personally observed a wide variety of activities available at each of the sites visited. Why was there a difference between the Site Supervisor Survey and our observations? Perhaps the terminology used in the survey instrument was ambiguous, the supervisors misreported activities on their survey, or our observations were not representative of the typical situation. If this last condition is true, Stone Soup sites not adhering well to this practice could improve by encouraging staff to make activities available to students more frequently if the equipment or materials are present. Of the types of activities considered, only those relating to science were consistently underprovided across programs. The monthly staff meetings present an opportunity for staff to share information on effective use of materials and equipment.

Features Distinguishing Sites Consistently Adhering to Practices Well or Poorly

As we had scores for each site across the set of practices, we sought to determine whether there were any distinguishing features of the programs that adhered consistently well to the range of practices we had identified. We had hoped that we could identify one or more administratively available variables that were statistically significant predictors of being a site that consistently adheres well (or poorly) to practices using multivariate regression. If successful, this would allow Stone Soup to extrapolate the results to all sites and to target those sites that are most likely to require resources and attention to improve their adherence to practices overall. Because of our small sample size, we were unable to estimate such a model and obtain stable coefficients. The next approach was to use basic bivariate statistics to identify correlates with consistent adherence to practices. However, none of the administrative information we had available (urban/rural site, enrollment, training) were significantly related to being a consistently strong or weak adherent to practices.

We should note that even if we had found a relationship between available administrative data and adherence to management practices, the policy prescription would not be immediately clear. For example, if sites with a college-educated site supervisor and better-educated staff performed consistently better than other sites, it could be that having a more educated site supervisor leads to closer adherence to management practices. Conversely, it may be that more educated staff are attracted to better-performing programs. In the first case, it would behoove the program to hire only college-educated site supervisors. In the second scenario, hiring college-educated site supervisors to work at lesser-adhering sites would not improve performance.

Recommendations for Monitoring Improvements in Adherence to Good Practices

We recommended to Stone Soup two alternative paths for future re-assessments of adherence to good practices, depending on the objective of the assessment. On the one hand, if Stone Soup wants to measure change overall in adherence to the 18 practices (or some subset thereof), it should replicate our study on a random sample of sites. However, this study would need to ensure confidentiality to the site respondents. Since there is only one site supervisor per site, if Stone Soup undertook this reassessment, it would need to administer the survey instrument to all site staff and ask them to respond anonymously. The resulting site score would be the average of all site staff reports. Alternatively, Stone Soup could contract with a third party to administer, collect, and complete the data entry for the sites. If Stone Soup wants to identify the sites needing the most improvement on specific practices, it can replicate the full study for all sites. This would obviously be a more expensive approach.

CAVEATS

Despite a careful review of the survey instruments with the Stone Soup board and president and with a pretest, it became apparent to us that in at least one instance a question was misunderstood by the respondents. Site supervisors were asked about the program evaluation process. The responses provided differed in general from the standard, centralized evaluation process that each of the sites undertake under the supervision of the central office. We suspect that at least some supervisors misinterpreted the term evaluation as referring to their own performance review. This example serves to highlight the importance of ensuring that all questions are properly directed and understood. In retrospect, we would have undertaken a more complete pretesting effort that involved asking respondents not only if they understood the questions but to tell us exactly how they interpret each question.

Our site visits were announced ahead of time, which may have caused some evaluation bias. Evaluation bias occurs when a site modifies normal behavior—i.e., are on their "best behavior." In several instances, we overheard children and nonstaff adults remarking that more materials or more staff were on hand than was ordinarily the case. Since adherence to the relevant practices (staff-to-child ratio and variety of activities) was in these two instances being measured through the surveys and not through observation, it was unlikely to have been affected. However, evaluation bias may have influenced practices such as providing enough quality materials, which was measured by observations during the site visits. To avoid this problem, we recommend that site visits be unannounced whenever possible.

The scaling system that we devised is imperfect and subject to criticism about what constitutes differing levels of adherence to good practices. A major problem we recognized after conducting the data collection is that our questions are "site-centric" and ignored management practices at the organizational level. For example, although Stone Soup has ties with a number of organizations and individuals who donate time and resources to the program, the individual sites were not credited for these ties unless the site supervisor reported them or had other site-specific ties. In this instance, if we were to conduct the study anew, we would credit Stone Soup programs for these organizational ties. In other cases, it is less clear how one should consider organizational-level practices. For example, the literature on the use of volunteers focuses on volunteers who have direct contact with children and can provide tutoring or reduce the student-to-staff ratio. If it is the presence of volunteers who interact directly with children that matters, then volunteers who staff the central office (but do not work at the sites) should not count at the site level. The literature in most cases still needs to clarify which management practices are important at the site level only and which matter at the organizational level in a case like Stone Soup. We do not consider these scales definitive but rather as an illustration of how survey reports can be summarized and presented in a useful way. As the after-school care literature develops, these and other scales can be refined.

Finally, in conjunction with Stone Soup, we decided to measure adherence to all 18 management practices for which there was relatively solid support in the literature. After the fact, it became apparent that some of Stone Soup's objectives are inconsistent with some of the practices. For instance, Stone Soup seeks to provide inexpensive care to every child in the community who needs it. This practice is contrary to the management practice of restricting total enrollment and thus is not an appropriate goal for Stone Soup. In other examples, sites have limited control over a practice (such as compensation, which is largely determined by the school district in our example). In assessing a program, evaluators need to be cognizant of practices that are inconsistent with a program's objectives and of those that may be beyond the control of a program.

Chapter Five

SUMMARY

Several long-term trends have led to increased interest on the part of the American public in how and where children spend their time after school: (1) a decline in the percentage of parents who stay at home, (2) recent highly publicized incidents of violence involving children and adolescents, and (3) a nationwide move toward academic accountability and increasing the role of after-school programs as a means of improving school performance. In response to these concerns, the number of after-school programs has steadily risen over the past decade. Increased federal and state funding suggests that the number of such programs will increase in the coming years.

With the sponsorship of Stone Soup Child Care Programs and additional support from the RAND Child Policy Project and the Promising Practices Network, we undertook an effort to (1) identify good after-school care management practices that available evidence and expert judgment indicate should be associated with quality care, and (2) carry out a case study to assess the degree to which Stone Soup's programs adhered to these good practices.

In accomplishing the first task, we assessed the research literature on after-school care in an effort to define good practices. By "good practices," we mean program or process elements that have been shown or upheld by experts in the field to be associated with high-quality after-school programs or with positive child outcomes (educational attainment, emotional development, health, etc.). Unfortunately, while the stronger empirical work we identified showed an association between practices and desirable outcomes, it failed to establish causal relationships. Most of the publications available for review are not empirical at all but summarize recommendations provided by expert panels, government agencies, advocacy groups, and individuals. Thus, judgment has played a strong role in our definition of good practices, and our list must be considered preliminary and subject to change in light of new research.

Our synthesis of the literature highlights the almost total lack of solid evidence available about what management practices matter in the provision of quality after-school care. In order to ensure that after-school care programs are structured such that they provide quality care (i.e., care that is linked to desirable outcomes), research needs to be undertaken that identifies management practices that matter.

In accomplishing our second task, we developed a measurement methodology and instruments to measure adherence to our list of practice standards and applied them to Stone Soup's child care programs. Stone Soup Child Care Programs is a nonprofit organization that administers school-based after-school programs in collaboration with local school districts, communities, and parents throughout California. The organization is supported by contributions from foundations, corporations and local businesses, government, and individuals.

We concluded that, on average, Stone Soup's programs do a solid job of adhering to good practices. To arrive at this conclusion, we collected administrative data from Stone Soup's central office, surveyed ten randomly chosen site supervisors, and visited those sites to supplement the information collected by survey. Based on this information, we rated each program's adherence to each of our good practices using scales that we derived or borrowed from existing instruments. This report provides the instruments we developed and the rating scales we used.

We present examples of the recommendations offered to Stone Soup for improvement specific to each standard (and to the standards where adherence was judged minimal). We also describe the limitations we encountered in our use of the instrument and scales and provide caveats for their potential users.

We hope that this application will prove useful for others seeking to measure adherence to after-school care management practices by providing a methodology and instruments that can be adopted as is or adapted to suit other applications.

LIST OF PUBLICATIONS REVIEWED

Table A.1 lists the author(s), title, year of publication, practices addressed, and report classification for each publication included in the meta-analysis. In this table, Tier 1 studies show a statistically significant relationship between the practice and a positive outcome. Tier 2 reports refer to recommendations regarding good management practices made by expert panels or derived from a literature review. Tier 3 studies are recommendations regarding practices in after-school care programs that were identified as being associated with beneficial outcomes or quality (without statistical support provided). Tier 4 articles refer to single-authored recommendations not expressly based on the experience of an after-school care program. Table A.2 lists the studies and reports that support each of the original 20 practices.

Table A.1

Practices and Methodology Category by Study

Author(s)	Title	Practices	Category
Albrecht, 1991	*Quality Criteria for School-Age Child Care Pro-grams*	Training staff Staff education Staff experience Staff compensation Variety of activities Flexibility of programming Emotional climate Child-to-staff ratio Total enrollment Mixing of age groups Age-appropriate activities Space and furnishings Clear goals and evaluation Materials Safety and health Involvement of families Use of volunteers Partnerships	Tier 2
Alexander, 1986	"School-Age Child Care: Concerns and Challenges"	Training staff Variety of activities Flexibility of programming Mixing of age groups	Tier 4
Baden et al., 1982	School-Aged Child Care: An Action Manual	Continuity and comple-mentarity	Tier 3
Belle, 1997	"Varieties of Self-Care: A Qualitative Look at Children's Experiences in the After-School Hours"	Staff turnover rate Variety of activities	Tier 3
California Department of Education, 1994	*Kids' Time: A School-Age Care Program Guide*	Variety of activities Age-appropriate activities Flexibility of programming Safety and health Involvement of families Partnerships Emotional climate	Tier 2
California Department of Education, 1996	*School-Age Care in California: Addressing the Needs of Children, Families, and Society*	Variety of activities Emotional climate Involvement of families Clear goals and evaluation Training staff	Tier 2

Table A.1 (continued)

Author(s)	Title	Practices	Category
		Space and furnishings Materials Clear goals and evaluation Training staff Continuity and comple- mentarity	
Carnegie Council on Adolescent Development, 1994	*Consultation on After-School Programs*	Emotional climate Variety of activities Safety and health Continuity and comple- mentarity Partnerships	Tier 2
Fashola, 1998	*Review of Extended-Day and After-School Programs and Their Effectiveness*	Training staff Involvement of families Clear goals and evaluation Flexibility of programming	Tier 2
Finn-Stevenson, Desimone, and Chung, 1998	*Linking Child Care and Support Services with the School: Pilot Evaluation of the School of the 21st Century*	Training staff Continuity and comple- mentarity Mixing of age groups	Tier 3 (preschool and before and after-school care)
Halpern, 1991	*The Role of After-School Programs in the Lives of Inner-City Children: A Study of the Urban Youth Network After-School Programs*	Safety and health Emotional climate Variety of activities Training staff Continuity and comple- mentarity Use of volunteers	Tier 3
Halpern, Spielberger, and Robb, 2000	*Evaluation of the MOST (Making the Most of Out-of-School Time) Initiative: Final Report*	Emotional climate Child-to-staff ratio Flexibility of programming Variety of activities Safety and health Space and furnishings Materials Clear goals and evaluation	Tier 3

Table A.1 (continued)

Author(s)	Title	Practices	Category
Huang et al., 2000	*A Decade of Results: The Impact of LA's Best After-School Enrichment Program on Subsequent Student Achievement and Performance*	Emotional climate Variety of activities	Tier 3
Kahne et al., 1999	"School and after-school programs as contexts for youth development: A Qualitative and Quantitative Assessment"	Continuity and complementarity	Tier 3
Miller and Marx, 1990	*After-School Arrangements in Middle Childhood: A Review of the Literature*	Safety and health Emotional climate Variety of activities Continuity and complementarity Involvement of families Partnerships Flexibility of programming Space and furnishings Training staff Age-appropriate activities	Tier 2
National Association of Elementary School Principals, 1999	*After-School Programs and the K–8 Principal: Standards for Quality School-Age Child Care*	Training staff Flexibility of programming Variety of activities Emotional climate Child-to-staff ratio Total enrollment Clear goals and evaluation Space and furnishings Continuity and complementarity Involvement of families Use of volunteers Safety and health Materials Staff turnover rate	Tier 2
National Institute on Out-of-School Time, 2000	*Making an Impact on Out-of-School Time*	Training staff Child-to-staff ratio Emotional climate	Tier 2

Table A.1 (continued)

Author(s)	Title	Practices	Category
		Variety of activities Safety and health Flexibility of programming Use of volunteers Clear goals and evaluation Continuity and comple- mentarity Partnerships Involvement of families	
National Re- search Council and Institute of Medicine, 2000	*After-School Pro- grams to Promote Child and Adoles- cent Development: Summary of a Workshop*	Training staff Staff compensation Space and furnishings Age-appropriate activities Emotional climate Flexibility of programming Mixing of age groups Clear goals and evaluation Materials Involvement of families Partnerships Safety and health	Tier 2
National School- Age Care Alliance, 1998	*The National School-Age Core Alliance: Stan- dards for Quality School-Age Care*	Training staff Staff education Staff experience Staff compensation Space and furnishings Age-appropriate activities Variety of activities Emotional climate Child to staff ratio Continuity and comple- mentarity Flexibility of programming Total enrollment Safety and health Materials Involvement of families Partnerships Clear goals and evaluation	Tier 2
Newman et al., 2000	*America's After- School Choice: The Prime Time for Ju- venile Crime, or Youth Enrichment and Achievement*	Child-to-staff ratio Emotional climate Variety of activities	Tier 2

Table A.1 (continued)

Author(s)	Title	Practices	Category
Pierce, Hamm, and Vandell, 1999	"Experiences in After-School Programs and Children's Adjustment in First-Grade Classrooms"	Emotional climate Flexibility of programming Variety of activities	Tier 1
RMC Corporation, 1993	*National Study of Before- and After-School Programs*	Staff education Space and furnishings Age-appropriate activities Variety of activities Emotional climate Child-to-staff ratio Total enrollment Involvement of families Materials Flexibility of programming	Tier 3
Rosenthal and Vandell, 1996	"Quality of Care at School-Aged Child-Care Programs: Regulatable Features, Observed Experiences, Child Perspectives, and Parent Perspectives"	Staff education Variety of activities Emotional climate Child-to-staff ratio Mixing of age groups Total enrollment	Tier 1
U.S. Departments of Education and Justice, 2000	*Working for Children and Families: Safe and Smart After-School Programs*	Training staff Staff education Staff experience Staff compensation Space and furnishings Age-appropriate activities Emotional climate Child-to-staff ratio Continuity and complementarity Clear goals and evaluation Materials Total enrollment Safety and health Involvement of families Partnerships Use of volunteers	Tier 2

Table A.1 (continued)

Author(s)	Title	Practices	Category
Walter, Caplan, and McElvain, 2000	*Beyond the Bell*	Training staff Staff compensation Variety of activities Continuity and comple- mentarity	Tier 2
Zigler and Lang, 1991	*Child Care Choices*	Child-to-staff ratio	Tier 2

Table A.2

Studies Referenced by Practice

Practice	Author(s)
Staff training	Albrecht
	Alexander
	California Department of Education (1994)
	California Department of Education (1996)
	Fashola
	Finn-Stevenson, Desimone, and Chung
	Halpern
	Miller and Marx
	National Association of Elementary School Principals
	National Institute on Out-of-School Time
	National Research Council and Institute of Medicine
	National School-Age Care Alliance
	U.S. Departments of Education and Justice
	Walter, Caplan, and McElvain
Staff education	Albrecht
	National School-Age Care Alliance
	RMC Corporation
	Rosenthal and Vandell
	U.S. Departments of Education and Justice
Staff turnover rate	Belle
	National Association of Elementary School Principals
Staff experience	Albrecht
	National School-Age Care Alliance
	U.S. Departments of Education and Justice
Staff compensation	Albrecht
	National Research Council and Institute of Medicine
	National School-Age Care Alliance
	U.S. Departments of Education and Justice
	Walter, Caplan, and McElvain
Variety of activities	Albrecht
	Alexander
	Belle
	California Department of Education (1994)
	California Department of Education (1996)
	Carnegie Council on Adolescent Development
	Halpern
	Halpern, Spielberger, and Robb
	Huang et al.
	Miller and Marx
	National Association of Elementary School Principals
	National Institute on Out-of-School Time

Table A.2 (continued)

Practice	Author(s)
	National School-Age Care Alliance
	Newman et al.
	Pierce, Hamm, and Vandell
	RMC Corporation
	Rosenthal and Vandell
	Walter, Caplan, and McElvain
Flexibility of programming	Albrecht
	Alexander
	California Department of Education (1994)
	Fashola
	Halpern, Spielberger, and Robb
	Miller and Marx
	National Association of Elementary School Principals
	National Institute on Out-of-School Time
	National Research Council and Institute of Medicine
	National School-Age Care Alliance
	Pierce, Hamm, and Vandell
	RMC Corporation
Emotional climate	Albrecht
	California Department of Education (1994)
	California Department of Education (1996)
	Carnegie Council on Adolescent Development
	Halpern
	Halpern, Spielberger, and Robb
	Huang et al.
	Miller and Marx
	National Association of Elementary School Principals
	National Institute on Out-of-School Time
	National Research Council and Institute of Medicine
	National School-Age Care Alliance
	Newman et al.
	Pierce, Hamm, and Vandell
	RMC Corporation
	Rosenthal and Vandell
	U.S. Departments of Education and Justice
Child-to-staff ratio	Albrecht
	Halpern, Spielberger, and Robb
	National Association of Elementary School Principals
	National Institute on Out-of-School Time
	National School-Age Care Alliance
	Newman et al.
	RMC Corporation
	Rosenthal and Vandell
	U.S. Departments of Education and Justice
	Zigler and Lang

Table A.2 (continued)

Practice	Author(s)
Total enrollment	Albrecht National Association of Elementary School Principals National School-Age Care Alliance RMC Corporation Rosenthal and Vandell U.S. Departments of Education and Justice
Mixing of age groups	Albrecht Alexander Finn-Stevenson, Desimone, and Chung National Research Council and Institute of Medicine Rosenthal and Vandell
Age-appropriate activities	Albrecht California Department of Education (1994) Miller and Marx National Research Council and Institute of Medicine National School-Age Care Alliance RMC Corporation U.S. Departments of Education and Justice
Space and furnishings available	Albrecht California Department of Education (1994) Halpern, Spielberger, and Robb Miller and Marx National Association of Elementary School Principals National Research Council and Institute of Medicine National School-Age Care Alliance RMC Corporation U.S. Departments of Education and Justice
Continuity and complementarity with day school programs	Baden, et al. California Department of Education (1994) Carnegie Council on Adolescent Development Finn-Stevenson, Desimone, and Chung Halpern Kahne et al. Miller and Marx National Association of Elementary School Principals National Institute on Out-of-School Time National School-Age Care Alliance U.S. Departments of Education and Justice Walter, Caplan, and McElvain
Clear goals and evaluation of program progress and effectiveness	Albrecht California Department of Education (1994) California Department of Education (1996) Fashola

Table A.2 (continued)

Practice	Author(s)
	Halpern, Spielberger, and Robb
	National Association of Elementary School Principals
	National Institute on Out-of-School Time
	National Research Council and Institute of Medicine
	National School-Age Care Alliance
	U.S. Departments of Education and Justice
Materials	Albrecht
	California Department of Education (1994)
	Halpern, Spielberger, and Robb
	National Association of Elementary School Principals
	National Research Council and Institute of Medicine
	National School-Age Care Alliance
	RMC Corporation
	U.S. Departments of Education and Justice
Attention to safety and health	Albrecht
	California Department of Education (1994)
	Carnegie Council on Adolescent Development
	Halpern
	Halpern, Spielberger, and Robb
	Miller and Marx
	National Association of Elementary School Principals
	National Institute on Out-of-School Time
	National Research Council and Institute of Medicine
	National School-Age Care Alliance
	U.S. Departments of Education and Justice
Involvement of families	Albrecht
	California Department of Education (1994)
	California Department of Education (1996)
	Fashola
	Miller and Marx
	National Association of Elementary School Principals
	National Institute on Out-of-School Time
	National Research Council and Institute of Medicine
	National School-Age Care Alliance
	RMC Corporation
	U.S. Departments of Education and Justice
Use of volunteers	Albrecht
	Halpern
	National Association of Elementary School Principals
	National Institute on Out-of-School Time
	U.S. Departments of Education and Justice

Table A.2 (continued)

Practice	Author(s)
Partnerships with community-based organizations, ju-venile justice agencies, law enforcement, and youth groups	Albrecht California Department of Education (1994) Carnegie Council on Adolescent Development Miller and Marx National Institute on Out-of-School Time National Research Council and Institute of Medicine National School-Age Care Alliance U.S. Departments of Education and Justice

SUMMARY OF STUDIES/REPORTS REVIEWED

This appendix briefly summarizes each of the publications included in the meta-analysis.

TIER I PUBLICATIONS

Pierce, Hamm, and Vandell (1999) studied the adjustment of 150 first-graders in 37 after-school programs by observing the children in the day care setting and in the classroom. Two practices were positively and statistically significantly related to children's adjustment in school: staff interactions and program flexibility. For boys, staff positivity (as expressed toward the children) was associated with boys' manifesting fewer internalizing and externalizing behaviors, and staff negativity was associated with boys' receiving poorer grades. Program flexibility was associated with boys' displaying better social skills. Availability of activities was based on observers' counting and assessing of the age appropriateness of activities offered. A low rating indicated few activities, limited in their developmental focus; a high rating reflected a wide choice of age-appropriate activities that focused on several developmental areas, including physical, social, and cognitive. Child adjustment outcomes were emotional and behavioral problems, academic grades, work habits, and social skills with peers. Child emotional and behavioral problems were assessed by the classroom teacher as "no problems," "internalization problems," and "externalization problems."

Rosenthal and Vandell (1996) investigated the relationship between program features and program quality. Larger staff-to-child ratios, lower staff education, and fewer program activities were each associated with a higher number of observed negative staff-child interactions. Children reported a poorer emotional climate in programs with larger total enrollment and those with a higher number of observed negative staff-child interactions; similarly, parents felt more positively toward programs with lower staff-to-child ratios and when their children reported a stronger emotional climate. All regulatable features (enrollment, number of staff and staff education, time on average that specific activities were offered) were reported by the program directors.[1] Program quality was assessed by participant and parent reports about the program and through interviewer-observed staff-child interactions about the program. Children's perceptions of the psychosocial climate of the after-school programs (including relationships with staff and other children in the center and perceptions about center's activities) were measured using the After-School Environmental Scale (ASES). The ASES is an instrument administered to children. Staff-child interactions were recorded using an adaptation of Vandell and Posner's (1995) observation system. The authors focus on the quality of after-school programs that serve school-age children between the third and fifth grades. A total of 180 children (94 in the third grade, 55 in the fourth grade, and 21 in the fifth grade) from 30 different programs gave their perceptions of their after-school programs.

TIER 2 PUBLICATIONS

Albrecht (1991), with the assistance of experts in the field, constructed a list of indicators of high quality for key program components. The criteria established by NAEYC for early-childhood programs were used as a starting point for these indicators of quality of school-age programs. These criteria were then amended and expanded by individuals and organizations with expertise in school-age care through discussions, workshops, panels, and feedback.

The *California School-Age Care Study* (California Department of Education, 1996), consisted of three components: (1) a statewide survey of over 1,000 programs; (2) in-depth interviews with 14 school-age care providers from five geographic locations throughout

---

[1]Observers also reported on staff-to-child ratios.

California, chosen to reflect diversity in ethnicity and socioeconomic status; and (3) discussions and analyses by members of the School-Age Care Advisory Committee. Respondents were asked for their input on what aspects of care are important to ensuring quality care.

The California Department of Education Child Development Division (1994), working in cooperation with the School-Age Care Working Group, developed a program guide for school-age care programs. A number of child care specialists representing a wide variety of programs contributed to the development of the guide. The document is intended for programs serving children from five to fourteen years of age. The guide outlines standards to be set and specifies what an exemplary school-age care program would look like.

The National Institute on Out-of-School Time (2000) prepared a guide on making the most impact on out-of-school time. They adapted quality indicators from the official National School-Age Care Alliance standards.

The National Research Council and Institute of Medicine published *After-School Programs to Promote Child and Adolescent Development: Summary of a Workshop* (2000), which brought together researchers, policymakers, and practitioners to discuss the current state of knowledge related to after-school care for children aged five to fourteen.

Newman et al. (2000) prepared a report for Fight Crime: Invest in Kids that reviews the after-school care literature and provides recommendations on how after-school care programs can achieve positive results in reducing juvenile crime. Fight Crime: Invest in Kids is a nonprofit national anticrime organization led by law enforcement personnel.

In *Working for Children and Families: Safe and Smart After-School Programs* (2000), the U.S. Departments of Education and Justice describe evidence showing that after-school care programs produce beneficial results and identify key components of after-school care programs that their experts believe are associated with quality care. The report also describes exemplary after-school care models throughout the nation.

Walter, Caplan, and McElvain (2000) interviewed after-school program practitioners about their perceptions of practices associated with high-quality after-school programs. These interviews were used to help develop a toolkit for "creating effective after-school programs" with a focus on management, collaboration, programming, evaluation, and communication issues.

The National Association of Elementary School Principals (1999), with the assistance of an advisory committee of principals, child care professionals, researchers, and organizations, prepared a set of standards for quality after-school age child care.

Fashola (1998) reviewed 34 evaluations of after-school programs and their relationship with child outcomes. The quality of the methodologies employed for the evaluations ranged from a randomized controlled experiment to self-evaluations. Fashola supplements the conclusions he draws from the review of the evaluation studies with a literature review. A major contribution was the identification of promising practices for after-school care.

The National School-Age Care Alliance (1998) Standards Committee developed the current version *Standards for Quality School-Age Care* on the basis of research and field testing in 75 programs in 13 states for accreditation purposes. All of the field-tested programs received training in the use of the Assessment of School-Age Child Care Quality (ASQ) self-study materials and the process of accreditation. This document includes recommendations based on pilot site experiences in addition to extensive reviews from the National School-Age Care Alliance Accreditation Advisory Board, National School-Age Care Alliance staff, and school-age care professionals around the country. The National School-Age Care Alliance standards for quality school-age care are divided into five categories: human relationships; indoor environment; outdoor environment; activities, safety, health, and nutrition; and administration. This is the major national accrediting body for school-age care.

The Carnegie Council on Adolescent Development working paper entitled *Consultation on After-School Development* (1994) was based on a 1994 workshop of the same name. The objective of the workshop was to explore the key issues in developing effective after-school programs and to identify federal strategies to promote high-quality programs nationwide.

Zigler and Lang (1991), in collaboration with several youth development organizations and individual experts, provide recommendations for quality child care, including after-school care.

Miller and Marx (1990) review the literature and compile a set of characteristics of school-age child care programs with a focus on identifying practices that address children's developmental needs.

TIER 3 PUBLICATIONS

In the *National Study of Before- and After-School Programs* (1993), RMC Corporation conducted 12 site visits to programs in three communities. The 12 programs vary in location, administration auspice, relatedness to public schools, quality features, and service to economically disadvantaged children. The quality of the programs was assessed using an adapted version of the ASQ observation tool, developed by the School-Age Child Care Project at Wellesley College. In an effort to more thoroughly understand the factors that influence quality ratings, the study examines connections between the telephone survey data, site visitors' observations, and interviews in search of factors correlating with program achievement on the ASQ. They compare ratings on human relationships, space, time allocation, and activities for the seven programs with the highest ASQ score with the five lowest-scoring programs. A nationally representative sample of 1,304 programs were interviewed by telephone. ASQ components were safety and health/nutrition, staff-child interactions, ratio and total enrollments, child-child interactions and staff-staff interactions (emotional climate), staff-parent interactions (involvement of families), space (indoor and outdoor), materials/supplies/equipment, flexibility of scheduling, variety of activities, and age-appropriate programming. This study is classified as Tier 3 (instead of Tier 1) because the ASQ scores were based on the practices rather than independently assessed. In other words, program practices are used to measure quality—they are not separate constructs.

Halpern, Spielberger, and Robb (2000) evaluated the MOST (Making the Most of Out-of-School Time) initiative. One component of the evaluation was the description and assessment of the "effectiveness of the MOST strategies to strengthen the quality of school-age care programs." Center quality for ten of the programs that were closely examined was based on observations. The authors draw the following conclusions: (1) the quality and number of materials boosted the morale of staff and children; (2) staff training led to improved management of selection of activities, room arrangement, schedule, and the like; (3) self-assessment compelled programs to set priorities and engage in self-reflection but was too time-consuming and disruptive for smaller, struggling programs; and (4) linking programs to external resources (e.g., organizations that offer volunteers or specialists or resource organizations) provided additional adjust into the program to teach and tutor the children, exposed children to new experiences, reduced the isolation that some programs felt, and sometimes provided staff additional training. These conclusions were based on the anecdotal reports of staff.

Huang et al. (2000) conducted a longitudinal study that evaluates the impact of participating in LA's BEST after-school care. The program now consists of 69 sites. Sites are selected on the basis of community need (assessed by local school performance, economic status of the community, and crime rates or gang activity). The program has been in existence for 12 years and caters free of charge to K–5 students. The UCLA Center for the Study of Evaluation studied the impact of participating in LA's BEST over four years compared with not participating. As part of the study, students and staff were interviewed about what components of the program worked and which could be improved. Staff and students mentioned that the availability of a variety of activities and the care and concern shown by staff were beneficial for the students.

Kahne et al. (1999) sampled 69 sixth- through tenth-grade students in three schools in Chicago participating in one of four after-school programs. Information was collected from surveys and observation. The paper recommends practices from an in-depth examination of the centers that provided the highest level of support for youth development. On the basis of the qualitative data, the authors identify coordination with the regular day school program as an important component of an effective program.

Finn-Stevenson, Desimone, and Chung (1998) evaluated the implementation of *two* pilot Schools of the 21st Century (21C). They compared the academic performance of children in the pilot after-school care programs with that of children not in the pilot programs. A second component of their evaluation (which we used) assessed the implementation of the after-school pilot programs via surveys administered to principals, teachers, and staff. From this evaluation, they derived ad hoc recommendations regarding the most effective practices. Principals and staff believed that (1) mixing age groups in the programs led to improved relationships among students of different ages and aided the children's personal growth and social development; (2) efforts to improve communication with regular day school teachers and to increase teacher involvement improved relations between staff and teachers; and (3) proper evaluation and feedback and the responsiveness of staff to this feedback are essential to improvement in quality of care.

Belle (1997) followed 53 families over time to understand changes in after-school care arrangements, a subset of which placed their children in after-school care programs. In other words, the empirical portion of this study examined changes in arrangements; it did not examine the associations between outcomes and specific characteristics of after-school programs. The paper included an in-depth case study of the experience of a single child in an after-school care program. Factors with which the parent and child reported concern were turnover rate and range of activities.

Halpern (1991) conducted an evaluation of the nine Urban Youth Network after-school programs in Chicago. He interviewed all site and center directors and 22 staff. He also conducted one-on-one interviews with 70 children and administered a survey to 650 children. Administrative data on activities and participation were examined. Although the study had no comparison group, it attempted to form nonempirical impressions about the programs' impact on children. The factors that were thought to influence quality included safety and health, offering a variety of activities, and the use of volunteers.

The School-Age Child Care Project (Baden et al., 1982), in collaboration with several youth development organizations and experts, compiled recommendations based on the experience of programs in

30 states, field research in 25 program sites, and original research on school-age child care. These recommendations were derived from the actual experience of the participants combined with original research (which did not meet the criteria for Tier 1 study). The one recommendation made in the report that relates to our practices is to reduce the "role ambiguity" of school-based after-school care staff by formally recognizing staff as part of the school community, including them in meetings, and encouraging coordination with teachers.

TIER 4 PUBLICATIONS

Alexander (1986) discusses the issues surrounding self-care of children during the after-school hours. She provides potential solutions to the latchkey problem, one of which includes after-school care centers. Finally, she discusses some characteristics that contribute to a center's success. These recommendations are not based on a systematic review of the literature; nor are they based on original empirical research.

SURVEY INSTRUMENTS

1, Goals/Objectives

This appendix shows the two instruments RAND designed to collect information from the Stone Soup central office and from the individual programs (via the on-site site supervisor). The site supervisors were guaranteed anonymity to ensure that we obtained as accurate a report as possible on the characteristics of the Stone Soup programs.

Stone Soup Survey for Specific Programs

School:_____

STUDENT ENROLLMENT

1. What is the total enrollment of students in the program for the 2000–2001 school year?
   _____NUMBER OF STUDENTS

2. How many students are enrolled in the following grades for the 2000–2001 school year?
   _____2nd grade and lower
   _____3rd and 4th grades
   _____5th grade
   _____6th grade and higher
   _____DON'T KNOW

STAFF BACKGROUND

The following questions relate to the Site Supervisor's background:

3. What is the highest level of education the Site Supervisor has completed? (CIRCLE RESPONSE)
   GRADUATE DEGREE
   BACHELOR'S DEGREE

ASSOCIATE DEGREE
CHILD DEVELOPMENT ASSOCIATE TRAINING
SOME COLLEGE, NO DEGREE
HIGH SCHOOL DIPLOMA OR GED
LESS THAN HIGH SCHOOL

4. Prior to his/her current job, did the Site Supervisor have any experience working with children? (CIRCLE RESPONSE)
    YES
    NO

5. Has the Site Supervisor participated in any school-age child-related training in the last year? (CIRCLE RESPONSE)
    YES
    NO   (SKIP TO QUESTION 7)

6. **(If yes)** What type of training did the Site Supervisor receive? For each type received, please circle the response indicating who paid for it: SS = Stone Soup, P = Site Supervisor personally, Both = Stone Soup and the Site Supervisor jointly paid for the training.

(Circle if training received) (Circle one)

First aid/CPR	SS	P	Both
Recognizing child abuse	SS	P	Both
Child development	SS	P	Both
Health and nutrition	SS	P	Both
Conflict resolution	SS	P	Both
Classroom management	SS	P	Both
Working with special-needs students	SS	P	Both
Multicultural awareness	SS	P	Both
Avoiding gender bias	SS	P	Both
Computer skills	SS	P	Both
Designing engaging activities	SS	P	Both
Budgeting/financial management	SS	P	Both
Data collection	SS	P	Both
Program evaluation	SS	P	Both
Curriculum training	SS	P	Both
Administration	SS	P	Both

Communication (with   SS   P   Both
    school personnel,
    parents)
Other (specify)   SS   P   Both

7.   What is the salary for this Site Supervisor? (Circle appropriate unit)

    $_____PER YEAR
             SCHOOL YEAR
             MONTH
             WEEK
             DAY
             HOUR

The following questions pertain to the Assistant in the program who has worked with the Stone Soup Programs the longest (i.e., the Assistant with the longest tenure):

8.   Prior to the Assistant's current job, had he/she worked with children before? (CIRCLE RESPONSE)

    YES
    NO
    DON'T KNOW

9.   Did the Assistant participate in any school-age child-related training in the last year? (CIRCLE RESPONSE)

    YES
    NO   (SKIP TO QUESTION 11)

10.   **(If yes)** What type of training did the Assistant receive? For each type received, please circle the response indicating who paid for it: SS = Stone Soup, P = Site Supervisor personally, Both = Stone Soup and the Assistant jointly paid for the training **(P and perhaps BOTH options may not be applicable)**.

(Circle if training received) (Circle one)

First aid/CPR	SS	P	Both
Recognizing child abuse	SS	P	Both
Child development	SS	P	Both
Health and nutrition	SS	P	Both
Conflict resolution	SS	P	Both
Classroom management	SS	P	Both
Working with special-needs students	SS	P	Both

Multicultural awareness	SS	P	Both
Avoiding gender bias	SS	P	Both
Computer skills	SS	P	Both
Designing engaging activities	SS	P	Both
Budgeting/financial management	SS	P	Both
Data collection	SS	P	Both
Program evaluation	SS	P	Both
Curriculum training	SS	P	Both
Administration	SS	P	Both
Communication (with school personnel, parents)	SS	P	Both
Other (specify)	SS	P	Both

11. What is the salary for this Assistant? (circle the appropriate unit)

$_____PER YEAR
          SCHOOL YEAR
          MONTH
          WEEK
          DAY
          HOUR

12. What fringe benefits do you provide for paid staff in this program who work with children? By fringe benefits we mean insurance, vacation time, sick time, and any other benefits they may receive. (**If your staff includes regular school teachers, *do not* include benefits they receive as teachers. Please circle all that apply.**)
NO BENEFITS
HEALTH INSURANCE
DENTAL INSURANCE
DISABILITY INSURANCE
LIFE INSURANCE
PAID VACATION TIME
PAID HOLIDAYS
PAID PERSONAL DAYS/BEREAVEMENT DAYS
"COMP" TIME
PAID SICK DAYS
RETIREMENT PENSION
FREE OR REDUCED-FEE CHILD CARE

TUITION SUPPORT
USE OF FACILITIES FREE OF CHARGE
OTHER (SPECIFY)

13. Do you require that all staff members be trained in first aid and CPR? (CIRCLE RESPONSE)
    YES
    NO
    DON'T KNOW

14. During the past 12 months, how many paid staff who work with children left this program? Include both full-time and part-time staff.
    _____ Staff

15. During the past 12 months, how many paid staff who work with children have been hired?
    _____ Staff

16. Thinking about the last time you had to fill a vacant paid staff position, how long was it from the time a staff member left to the time a replacement was hired for this program? **Do not count time when the program is not operating (e.g., summer vacation).**
    (Circle appropriate unit)
    _____   DAYS
               WEEKS
               MONTHS
               YEARS
               IMMEDIATELY
               DON'T KNOW

Site Supervisor Survey

Dear Site Supervisor,

The Stone Soup Child Care Programs has requested that RAND measure Stone Soup's adherence to best practices in a sample of their after-school programs. Your candid responses regarding the program will greatly enhance the accuracy of the results. We have a few points that we would like to emphasize:

Please fill out this survey before our site visit arranged for _____. At that time, a RAND researcher will pick up the survey.

Your responses are confidential. We will aggregate and report responses to the Stone Soup program, but we will not release any information linking you or your specific program to your responses.

Not all of the questions on this survey will pertain to your program.

Please mark your responses or fill in the blanks for the following questions. All questions pertain to the after-school care program.

Please circle or fill in your responses. The first set of questions pertains to the types of activities offered in your program.

ACTIVITIES
1. Does the program regularly offer a variety of activities? (CIRCLE RESPONSE)
     YES
     NO
     DON'T KNOW
2. Are these activities age-appropriate? (CIRCLE RESPONSE)
     YES
     NO
     DON'T KNOW

3. On a typical day, which of these activities do the students have available to them? For each activity, please indicate whether it is *offered* daily, weekly, monthly, occasionally, or as needed by checking the appropriate box. (By offered, we mean available for children to participate in or use.)	Daily	Weekly	Monthly	Occa-sionally	As Needed	Don't Know
ACTIVITY						
A. Create arts or crafts such as painting, sewing, or carpentry						
B. Construction or building with hollow blocks, Lego™, or sand						
C. Science activities or experiments						
D. Board or card games, puzzles						
E. Reading independently or in small groups						
F. Creative writing						
G. Time for doing homework						
H. Computer electronic games						
I. Television watching						

J. Video or movie viewing					
K. Cooking food or preparation					
L. Unstructured dramatic play or dress-up play					
M. Storytelling, role playing, or theatrical activities					
N. Movement, dance, or exercise activities					
O. Music making, music appreciation or singing activities					
P. Unstructured physically active play such as running or swimming					
Q. Organized individual skill-building sports such as swimming, track, field, gymnastics					
R. Organized team sports such as soccer					
S. Field trips, excursions					
T. Socializing					
U. Tutoring					
V. Formal guidance or psychological counseling or therapy					
W. Free time					

X. Referrals to counseling					
Y. Nutrition classes					
Z. Other (SPECIFY)					

4. What special previsions do you make for children over age 9?
(CIRCLE ALL THAT APPLY)
SEPARATE SPACE
DIFFERENT AGE-APPROPRIATE ACTIVITIES
ACTIVITIES IN THE COMMUNITY
HELPING WITH YOUNGER CHILDREN
WORK EXPERIENCE
LONGER-TERM ACTIVITIES (e.g., PLAYS, ARTS AND CRAFTS
PROJECTS)
OWN CLUB PROGRAM
OTHER (SPECIFY)_____

_____

5. Do younger (K–3 grades) and older children (4th grade and
above) interact (e.g., do they share the playground at the same
time)? (CIRCLE RESPONSE)
     YES
     NO
     DON'T KNOW

6. Do older children (4th grade and above) mentor or act as role
models for younger children (K–3) (e.g., tutoring or leading
games)? (CIRCLE RESPONSE)
     YES
     NO
     DON'T KNOW

EQUIPMENT AND MATERIALS

7. What is the condition of the materials and equipment (e.g.,
games, toys, books, etc.) that the children use? (CIRCLE
RESPONSE)
     EXCELLENT
     GOOD
     FAIR
     POOR
     DON'T KNOW

8. Are most of the games and other toys missing pieces? (CIRCLE
RESPONSE)
     YES
     NO
     DON'T KNOW

9.   Do you have enough age-appropriate equipment for all children? (CIRCLE RESPONSE)
        YES
        NO
        DON'T KNOW

SNACKS

10   Does the program provide a snack to children? (CIRCLE RESPONSE)
11.   If yes, how frequently is the snack provided? (CIRCLE RESPONSE)
12.   If the program provides a snack, what is the snack(s)? (PLEASE FILL IN)
13.   If you do not provide a snack, do you provide time when children can eat snacks they bring from home? (CIRCLE RESPONSE)
        YES
        NO
        DON'T KNOW

SAFETY

14.   Do you have a system for signing students in and out of the program? (CIRCLE RESPONSE)
        YES
        NO
        DON'T KNOW
15.   If the child is absent, which of the following actions do you take? (CIRCLE ALL THAT APPLY)
        Contact the parent/guardian
        Contact the school
        Other (SPECIFY)_____
        _____
        No action
        DON'T KNOW

STAFF MENTORING

16.   Do you have any mentoring system for new staff (e.g., assigning new staff to more senior staff mentors)? (CIRCLE RESPONSE)
        YES
        NO   (SKIP TO QUESTION 18)
17.   Is the mentoring system formal or informal (CIRCLE RESPONSE)
        FORMAL
        INFORMAL

INTERACTIONS BETWEEN AFTER-SCHOOL STAFF AND REGULAR SCHOOL FACULTY

18. Do after-school staff attend regular school faculty meetings? (CIRCLE RESPONSE)
    YES
    NO

19. If yes, how frequently do they attend? (CIRCLE RESPONSE)
    RARELY
    OCCASIONALLY
    FREQUENTLY
    ALWAYS

20. Do after-school staff and day school faculty regularly communicate about students' achievement and behavior? (CIRCLE RESPONSE)
    YES
    NO
    DON'T KNOW

21. Do staff and faculty communicate about lesson plans and activities? (CIRCLE RESPONSE)
    YES
    NO
    DON'T KNOW

COMMUNICATION WITH PARENTS

22. How do you typically communicate with parents about their child's care and activities? (CIRCLE ALL THAT APPLY)
    REGULAR CONFERENCES
    PHONE CALLS
    NEWSLETTER
    SEND NOTES OR LETTERS HOME WITH CHILDREN
    TALK TO PARENTS WHEN DROPPING OFF OR PICKING
      UP CHILD
    E-MAIL
    OTHER (SPECIFY)_____

    _____
    DON'T KNOW

23. IF PROGRAM HAS REGULAR CONFERENCES WITH PARENTS: How often are parent conferences typically schedules (CIRCLE UNIT)
    |__|__|__| TIMES PER YEAR
                MONTH
                WEEK
                DAY
                AS NEEDED
                DON'T KNOW

USE OF COMMUNITY RESOURCES

24. Do you use community facilities? (CIRCLE RESPONSE)

YES
NO   (SKIP TO QUESTION 26)
DON'T KNOW   (SKIP TO QUESTION 26)

25.   Which facilities? (CIRCLE ALL THAT APPLY)
        LIBRARY
        PARKS
        COMMUNITY CENTERS
        SWIMMING POOL
        OTHER (SPECIFY)

26.   Do you partner with civic clubs, social service agencies, or religious organizations to provide community service activities for children? (CIRCLE RESPONSE)
        YES
        NO
        DON'T KNOW

27.   Are community members invited to the program to share talents or expertise? (CIRCLE RESPONSE)
        YES
        NO   (SKIP TO QUESTION 29)
        DON'T KNOW   (SKIP TO QUESTION 29)

28.   How often (weekly, monthly)? (CIRCLE RESPONSE)
        WEEKLY
        MONTHLY
        OCCASIONALLY
        DON'T KNOW

SPACE

29.   What spaces are regularly used by your after-school program? (CIRCLE ALL THAT APPLY)
        TRAILERS
        GYM
        CAFETERIA/MULTIPURPOSE OR ALL-PURPOSE ROOM
        ART ROOM
        MUSIC ROOM
        LIBRARY
        CLASSROOM
        PLAYGROUND/PARK
        GAME ROOM
        BASEMENT
        OFFICE
        ALL ROOMS IN SCHOOL
        OTHER (SPECIFY)_____
        _____
        DON'T KNOW

30. Do you have any problems with the space where your program is located? (CIRCLE RESPONSE)

      YES

      NO   (SKIP TO QUESTION 32)

      DON'T KNOW   (SKIP TO QUESTION 32)

31. What problems do you have with the space where the program is located? (CIRCLE ALL THAT APPLY)

      HAVE TO RELOCATE

      HAVE TO SHARE IT

      DON'T HAVE (ENOUGH) STORAGE SPACE

      LACK OF OFFICE SPACE

      LIMITED USE OF EQUIPMENT

      MUST REARRANGE THE ROOM AT THE
        BEGINNING/END OF EACH DAY

      EQUIPMENT NOT AGE-APPROPRIATE

      PLAYGROUND INADEQUATE

      POOR LIGHT, HEAT, OR VENTILATION

      NOISE

      SECURITY/VANDALISM

      LIMITED ACCESS TO TELEPHONE

      NO ROOM TO EXPAND

      NOT ENOUGH SPACE FOR ACTIVITIES

      OTHER (SPECIFY)_____

_____

      DON'T KNOW

32. Do you always have at least one staff member present who is trained in first aid and CPR?

      YES

      NO

      DON'T KNOW

33. On an average day, including yourself, how many paid after-school staff have direct contact with children? (Include both full-time and part-time staff.)

      _____Staff

FAMILY INVOLVEMENT

34. Do parents participate in planning and/or evaluating the program? (CIRCLE RESPONSE)

      YES

      NO

      SOMETIMES

35. Do parents serve on an advisory council or board of directors for the program? (CIRCLE RESPONSE)

      YES

      NO

36. Are there any other major ways that parents are involved with the program? (CIRCLE RESPONSE)
    YES
    NO   (SKIP TO QUESTION 38)

37. What are the other major ways that parents are involved with the program? (CIRCLE ALL THAT APPLY).
    ATTEND CHILDREN'S PROGRAMS
    FIELD TRIPS
    SERVE AS VOLUNTEERS
    CHOOSE ACTIVITIES
    SELECT STAFF
    REVIEW BUDGETS
    RAISE FUNDS
    BUILDING MAINTENANCE
    ATTEND WORKSHOPS
    ATTEND PARENT MEETINGS
    SET POLICY
    OTHER (SPECIFY)_____
    _____

38. Is any parent involvement *required* for your program? (CIRCLE RESPONSE)
    YES
    NO

EVALUATION AND FORMAL REVIEW

39. Is your after-school program reviewed or evaluated at least once a year? (CIRCLE RESPONSE)
    YES
    NO   (SKIP TO QUESTION 42)

40. Is this review formal, informal, or both formal and informal? (Informal means that comments are provided orally and informally by staff, director, or parents. No formal report is prepared.) (CIRCLE RESPONSE)
    INFORMAL ONLY   (SKIP TO QUESTION 42)
    FORMAL ONLY
    INFORMAL AND FORMAL
    DON'T KNOW   (SKIP TO QUESTION 42)

41. Who reviews your program? (CIRCLE ALL THAT APPLY)
    PROGRAM STAFF
    PARENTS
    NATIONAL ORGANIZATION STAFF
    FUNDING ORGANIZATION STAFF
    BOARD OF EDUCATION/SCHOOL DISTRICT STAFF
    OTHER (SPECIFY)_____
    _____

VOLUNTEER PARTICIPATION IN THE PROGRAM

42. Does your program use any volunteers? (CIRCLE RESPONSE)
    YES
    NO   (SKIP TO QUESTION 50)

43. Do these volunteers interact directly with the children?
    (CIRCLE RESPONSE)
    YES
    NO
    DON'T KNOW

44. Do you actively recruit volunteers? (CIRCLE RESPONSE)
    YES
    NO   (SKIP TO QUESTION 46)
    DON'T KNOW   (SKIP TO QUESTION 46)

45. Where do you recruit volunteers from? (CIRCLE ALL THAT
    APPLY)
    COLLEGES AND UNIVERSITIES
    NEIGHBORHOOD
    SCHOOLS
    COMMUNITY ORGANIZATIONS
    STUDENT FAMILY MEMBERS
    RELIGIOUS ORGANIZATIONS
    OTHER (SPECIFY)_____
    _____
    DON'T KNOW

46. If volunteers work with the children, does Stone Soup provide
    orientation or training before they begin working with the
    children? (CIRCLE RESPONSE)
    YES
    NO
    DON'T KNOW

47. Does Stone Soup conduct background checks on volunteers?
    (IF YES, CIRCLE TYPE OF CHECKS)
    YES
       REFERENCE CHECK
       MEGAN'S LAW
    NO
    DON'T KNOW

48. How many volunteers do you have signed up to work for the
    school year 2000–2001?
          _____ NUMBER OF VOLUNTEERS
    DON'T KNOW

49. On an average school day, how many volunteers are present to
    work with the children?

_____ NUMBER OF VOLUNTEERS
DON'T KNOW

YOUR OPINION OF THE STONE SOUP CHILD CARE PROGRAM

(50.) In your opinion, what are the three strongest features of the
Stone Soup Child Care Program?

1. _____
2. _____
3. _____

(51.) In your opinion, what are the three weakest features of the
Stone Soup Child Care Program?

1. _____
2. _____
3. _____

Afterschool Alliance, "Comparison Chart on 21st Century in House and Senate Versions of ESEA Reauthorization Bills (H.R. 1)," http://www.afterschoolalliance.org/esea_chart.cfm, 2001.

Albrecht, Kay M., *Quality Criteria for School-Age Child Care Programs*, Virginia: American Home Economics Association, 1991.

Alexander, Nancy P., "School-Age Child Care: Concerns and Challenges," *Young Children*, Vol. 42, 1986, pp. 3–10.

Austin, D., "Formal Educational Preparation: The Structural Prerequisite to the Professional Status of the Child Care Worker," *Child Care Quarterly*, Vol. 10, 1981, pp. 250–260.

Baden, Ruth Kramer, et al., *School-Age Child Care: An Action Manual*, Westport, CT: Auburn House Publishing Company, 1982.

Belle, Deborah, "Varieties of Self-Care: A Qualitative Look at Children's Experiences in the After-School Hours," *Merrill-Palmer Quarterly*, Vol. 43, No. 3, 1997, pp. 478–496.

Berk, L., and M. Berson, "A Review of the Child Development Associate Credential," *Child Care Quarterly*, Vol. 10, 1981, pp. 9–42.

California Department of Education, Child Development Division, *Kids' Time: A School-Age Care Program Guide*, Sacramento, CA, 1994.

California Department of Education, *School-Age Care in California: Addressing the Needs of Children, Families and Society,* Sacramento, CA, 1996.

Canadian Task Force on the Periodic Health Examination, "The Periodic Health Examination," *Canadian Medical Association Journal,* Vol. 121, No. 9, 1979, pp. 1193–1254.

Cappizzano, Jeffrey, Kathryn Tout, and Gina Adams, "Child Care Patterns of School-Age Children with Employed Mothers, *Assessing the New Federalism,* Occasional Paper No. 41, Washington, D.C.: The Urban Institute Press, 2000.

Carnegie Council on Adolescent Development, *Consultation on After-School Programs,* New York: Carnegie Corporation of New York, 1994.

Cost, Quality, and Outcomes Study Team, *Cost, Quality, and Child Outcomes in Child Care Centers, Public Report,* Denver, CO: University of Colorado Department of Economics, 1995.

Fashola, Olatokunbo S., *Review of Extended-Day and After-School Programs and Their Effectiveness,* Baltimore, MD: Center for Research on the Education of Students Placed at Risk, 1998.

Finn-Stevenson, Matia, Laura Desimone, and An-Me Chung, *Linking Child Care and Support Services with the School: Pilot Evaluation of the School of the 21st Century,* New Haven, CT: Yale University Bush Center in Child Development and Social Policy, 1998.

Halpern, Robert, *The Role of After-School Programs in the Lives of Inner-City Children: A Study of the Urban Youth Network After-School Programs,* Chicago, IL: Chapin Hall Center for Children at the University of Chicago, 1991.

Halpern, Robert, Julie Spielberger, and Sylvan Robb, *Evaluation of the MOST (Making the Most of Out-of-School Time) Initiative: Final Report,* Chicago, IL: Chapin Hall Center for Children at the University of Chicago, 2000.

Harms, T., E. V. Jacobs, and D. R. White, *School-Age Care Environment Rating Scale*, New York: Columbia University, Teachers College, 1996.

Huang, Denise, Barry Gribbons, Kyung Sung Kim, Charlotte Lee, and Eva L. Baker, *A Decade of Results: The Impact of the LA's BEST After-School Enrichment Program on Subsequent Student Achievement and Performance*, Los Angeles: CA: UCLA Center for the Study of Evaluation, 2000.

Kahne, Joseph, Jenny Nagaoka, Andrea Brown, James O'Brien, Therese Quinn, and Keith Thandiede, "School and After-School Programs as Contexts for Youth Development: A Qualitative and Quantitative Assessment," in Margaret C. Wang and William Lowe Boyd, eds., *Improving Results for Children and Families: Linking Collaborative Services with School Reform Efforts*, Oakland, CA: Mills College Department of Education, 1999.

Kisker, E. E., S. L. Hofferth, A. Brayfield, S. G. Deich, and P. Holcomb, *A Profile of Child Care Settings: Early Education and Care in 1990*, Washington, D.C.: U.S. Department of Education, 1991.

Mazzuca, S., "Does Patient Education in Chronic Disease Have Therapeutic Value?" *Journal of Chronic Diseases*, Vol. 3, 1982, pp. 521–529.

Miller, Beth Midzik, and Fern Marx, *After-School Arrangements in Middle Childhood: A Review of the Literature* (Action Research Paper No. 2), Wellesley, MA: Wellesley College Center for Research on Women, School-Age Child Care Project, 1990.

Morris, Darrell, Beverly Shaw, and Jan Perney, "Helping Low Readers in Grades 2 and 3: An After-School Volunteer Tutoring Program," *Elementary School Journal*, Vol. 91, No. 2, 1990, pp. 135–150.

Mulrow, C. D., D. J. Cook, and F. Davidoff, "Systematic Reviews: Critical Links in the Great Chain of Evidence," in C. Mulrow and D. Cook, eds., *Systematic Reviews: Synthesis of Best Evidence for Health Care Decisions*, Philadelphia, PA: American College of Physicians, 1998.

National Association of Elementary School Principals, *After-School Programs and the K–8 Principal: Standards for Quality School-Age Child Care*, revised edition, Alexandria, VA: National Association of Elementary School Principals, 1999.

National Institute on Out-of-School Time, *Making an Impact on Out-of-School Time*, Wellesley, MA: Wellesley College Center for Research on Women, National Institute on Out-of-School Time, 2000.

National Research Council and Institute of Medicine, *After-School Programs to Promote Child and Adolescent Development: Summary of a Workshop*, Jennifer A. Gootman, ed., Washington, D.C.: National Academy Press, 2000.

National School-Age Care Alliance, *The National School-Age Care Alliance Standards for Quality School-Age Care*, Boston, MA, 1998.

Newman, Sanford A., James Alan Fox, Edward A. Flynn, and William Christeson, *America's After-School Choice: The Prime Time for Juvenile Crime, or Youth Enrichment and Achievement*, Washington, D.C.: Fight Crime: Invest in Kids, 2000.

Pierce, Kim M., Jill V. Hamm, and Deborah Lowe Vandell, "Experiences in After-School Programs and Children's Adjustment in First-Grade Classrooms," *Child Development*, Vol. 80, No. 3, 1999, pp. 756–767.

RMC Corporation, *National Study of Before- and After-School Programs*, Final Report to the Office of Policy and Planning, Washington, D.C.: U.S. Department of Education, 1993.

Rosenthal, Robert, and Deborah Lowe Vandell, "Quality of Care at School-Aged Child Care Programs: Regulatable Features, Observed Experiences, Child Perspectives, and Parent Perspectives," *Child Development*, Vol. 67, 1996, pp. 2434–2445.

Shekelle, Paul G., and Sally C. Morton, "Principles of Metaanalysis," *Journal of Rheumatology*, Vol. 27, No. 1, 2000, pp. 251–253.

U.S. Departments of Education and Justice, *Working for Children and Families: Safe and Smart After-School Programs*, Washington, D.C.: U.S. Government Printing Office, 2000.

Vandell, Deborah Lowe, and K. M. Pierce, *Experiences in After-School Programs and Children's Well-Being*, paper presented to the Society for Research in Child Development, 2001.

Vandell, Deborah Lowe, and Jill K. Posner, *An Ecological Analysis of the Effects of After-School Care*, final report to the Spencer Foundation, 1995.

Walter, Katie E., Judith G. Caplan, and Carol K. McElvain, *Beyond the Bell*, Naperville, IL: North Central Regional Educational Laboratory, 2000.

Whitebook, Marcy, Carollee Howes, and Deborah Phillips, *Who Cares? Child Care Teachers and the Quality of Care in America*, final report, National Child Care Staffing Study, Oakland, CA: Child Care Employee Project, 1989.

Whitebook, Marcy, Deborah Phillips, and Carollee Howes, *National Child Care Staffing Study Revisited: Four Years in the Life of Center-Based Care*, Oakland, CA: Child Care Employee Project, 1993.

Wolf, Fredric M., *Meta-Analysis: Quantitative Methods for Research Analysis*, Newbury Park, CA: Sage Publications, 1986.

Zigler, Edward F., and Mary E. Lang, *Child Care Choices*, New York: The Free Press, 1991.